Rights, Roles and Responsibilities at School

A unit exploring the responsibilities of various school roles, including students' own responsibilities, in helping to meet students' needs

Authors

Mara Coward

Susan Johnson

Roberta MacQuarrie

Mary Mulleady

Patti Taunton

Cara Tole

Susan Whyte

May Wong

Lynn Zuehlke

Illustrator

Danna deGroot

Editors

Maureen McDermid

Mary Abbott

Roland Case

The Critical
Thinking Cooperative

BRITISH
COLUMBIA

Series published by

The Critical Thinking Cooperative
Richmond School District
7811 Granville Ave.
Richmond, British Columbia V6Y 3E3
tel: 604-668-6069; fax: 604-668-6191
e-mail: mmcdermid@richmond.sd38.bc.ca

Cover design: Antonio Banyard
Interior design: M. Kathie Wraight, Field Programs, Simon Fraser University
Production: Carpe Diem Educational Consulting, Inc.
Cover photograph: © Vancouver School Board; Josh Benson, photographer, 2002

National Library of Canada Cataloguing in Publication Data

Main entry under title:

Rights, roles and responsibilities at school : a unit exploring the
responsibilities of various school roles, including students' own
responsibilities, in helping to meet other students' needs / authors,
Mara Coward ... [et al.] ; editors, Maureen McDermid, Mary Abbott,
Roland Case.

(Critical challenges across the curriculum series, ISSN 1205-9730)
Co-published by: Ministry of Education, British Columbia.
Includes bibliographical references.
ISBN 0-86491-248-X

  1. Critical thinking--Study and teaching (Primary) 2. Conduct of
life--Study and teaching (Primary) 3. Life skills--Study and teaching
(Primary). I. Case, Roland, 1951- II. Abbott, Mary, 1950- III.
Coward, Mara. IV. British Columbia. Ministry of Education. V. Critical
Thinking Cooperative. VI. Series.
LB1590.3.R53 2003   158.2'0834   C2003-910309-9

Introductions

Critical Challenges

Blackline Masters

Table of Contents

Critical Challenges Across the Curriculum is an ongoing series of teacher resources focussed on infusing critical thinking into every school subject. Two features distinguish this series from the many other publications that support critical thinking—our *content-embedded* approach and our emphasis on *teaching the intellectual tools*.

Our approach is to embed critical thinking by presenting focussed questions or challenges that invite critical student reflection about the content of the curriculum. We do not see critical thinking as a generic set of skills or processes that can be developed independently of content and context. Nor do we believe that critical thinking can be adequately addressed as an add-on to the curriculum. Rather, critical thinking is profitably viewed as a way to teach the content of the curriculum. Teachers can help students understand the subject matter, as opposed to merely recalling it, by providing continuing opportunities for thoughtful analysis of issues that are central to the curriculum.

The second distinguishing feature of this series is its emphasis on systematically teaching a full range of tools for critical thinking. Much of the frustration that teachers experience when inviting students to think critically stems from students' lack of the relevant intellectual tools. No doubt some students will figure things out for themselves, but most of the rest will perform at higher levels only if they are taught the requisite tools for the job. For this reason, every critical challenge is accompanied with a list of the tools needed to respond competently, and considerable attention is paid in the suggested activities to detailing how these tools may be taught and assessed.

The British Columbia Ministry of Education has greatly contributed to our work through grants to Richmond, Delta and Maple Ridge school districts to support the efforts of 23 teams of educators associated with TC^2 partners around the province. Over the past two years, through Networks in Teacher Development in Social Studies projects, teachers at all levels have been creating and piloting materials in social studies using a critical thinking approach. The upshot of their efforts is a substantial collection of teacher-developed resources that involve students in thinking critically about social studies, and that teach them the tools to do this well.

We are especially pleased that the Ministry, as part of its larger initiative to support social studies in British Columbia, is sponsoring publication of twelve resources in this series—one for each grade level from kindergarten to grade 11.

We join with the Ministry in hoping that teachers will find these resources of use in their ongoing efforts to make social studies a critically thoughtful, engaging and valuable subject.

Roland Case and LeRoi Daniels

Series Editors

Many people have contributed to the project that has made publication of this resource possible. Maureen McDermid deserves enormous credit for coordinating our efforts. We thank Bruce Beairsto (Richmond), Steve Cardwell (Delta) and Lindy Jones (Maple Ridge) for their leadership and Mary Abbott, LeRoi Daniels, Elaine Decker, Patricia Finlay, Karyl Mills and Neil Smith for help in facilitating the project. We appreciate Shelley Hallock's and Linda Farr Darling's much needed proofreading. The Vancouver Foundation's financial support of this project was both generous and greatly appreciated. And finally we are indebted to the hundreds of educators who contributed their time and efforts to developing and piloting resources, and to the team leaders listed below who supported these dedicated educators over the past two years.

	Partner representatives	*Team mentors*
Abbotsford District #34	Bruce Mills	Karen Saenger Tina Hinds
BC Intermediate Teachers' Association	Paul Wood	Dorothea Hines
BC Primary Teachers' Association	Bonnie Jesten	Carolyn Edwards
BC Social Studies Teachers' Association	Wayne Axford	Violet Columbara
BC Teacher-Librarians' Association	Mark Roberts Joan Eaton	Bonnie McComb
Burnaby District #41	Mat Hassen	Lisa Schultz
Central Okanagan District #23	Mike Roberts	Wally Swarchuk
Coast Mountain District #82	Sharon Beedle	Christine Foster
Delta District #37	Steve Cardwell	Cheryl Norman Sandra Peel
Greater Victoria District #61	Tanis Carlow	Harry Lewis Tim Bradshaw
Malaspina University College	Mike Grant	Neil Smith
Maple Ridge District #42	Lindy Jones	Patti Taunton
Nanaimo District #68	Leona Kyrytow	Mary-Lynn Epps Leona Kyrytow
North Vancouver District #44	Cathy Molinski	Sandra Kinnon
Okanagan Similkameen #53	Jim Insley	Greg Smith Barbra Paterson
Prince Rupert District #52	Leah Robinson	Leah Robinson
Richmond District #38	Betty Eades	Mike Perry-Whittingham Catriona Misfeldt
Saanich District #63	Sheila Miller	Susan McRae
Simon Fraser University	Roland Case	Roland Case
Surrey District #36	Sherri Mohoruk	Alice Tiles
University of British Columbia	Linda Farr Darling	Linda Farr Darling
Vancouver District #39	Frank McCormick	Phyllis Schwartz
West Vancouver District #45 & West Vancouver Teachers' Association	Geoff Jopson	Bronwen Gouws

Each **critical challenge** is a **question** or **task** which is the focal activity upon which the lesson is based. An **overview** describes the topic and the main activities that students undertake.

Broad understanding is the intended curricular understanding that will emerge as students work through the challenge.

Requisite tools provide an inventory of specific intellectual resources that students need to competently address the critical challenge:

 Background knowledge — the information about the topic required for thoughtful reflection;

 Criteria for judgment — the considerations or grounds for deciding which of the alternatives is the most sensible or appropriate;

 Critical thinking vocabulary — the concepts and distinctions that help to think critically about the topic;

 Thinking strategies — procedures, organizers, models or algorithms that help in thinking through the challenge;

 Habits of mind — the values and attitudes of a careful and conscientious thinker that are especially relevant to the critical challenge.

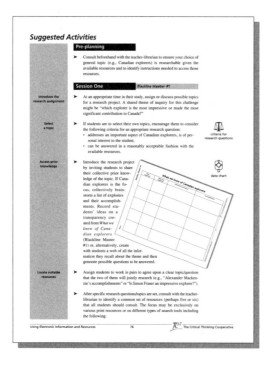

The body of the lesson is found under **suggested activities** which indicate how the critical challenge may be introduced and how the requisite tools may be taught.

Where relevant, **sessions** indicate where each anticipated new lesson would begin and the blackline masters needed for that session.

Down the left-hand panel is a handy **summary of main tasks** or activities for each session.

Icons along the right-hand side point out where specific tools are addressed.

Also provided in **evaluation** are assessment criteria and procedures, and in **extension** are found suggestions for further exploration or broader application of key ideas.

References cited in the suggested activities or recommended for additional information are often listed.

Blackline masters *follow each lesson. These are the reproducible learning resources referred to in the suggested activities. They serve a wide range of purposes:*

- **assessment rubrics** *identify suggested criteria and standards for evaluating student work;*

- **briefing sheets** *provide background information for students;*

- **data charts** *contain various organizers for recording and analysing information;*

- **documents** *refer to primary source material including paintings and other illustrations;*

- **student activities** *provide questions and tasks for students to complete;*

- **transparencies** *refer to material that can be converted to a transparency for use on an overhead projector.*

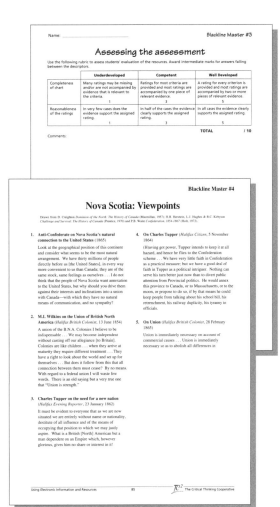

Electronic sourcebook *is a web-based supplement to our print publications. These materials include colour reproductions of pictures, primary documents, and updated links to other sites.*

- *If electronic resources had been developed at the time of publication, the available resources are referenced in the Suggested Activities.*

- *Periodically we update or supplement the print volumes with additional electronic information and resources.*

To locate referenced materials or to see whether new material has been developed, access our website and look for the title of this publication under the Electronic Sourcebook *heading (www.tc2.ca/pub/sourcebook).*

For more information about our model of critical thinking consult our website — www.tc2.ca.

Exploring needs and wants

 Objects have needs

3 sessions

This challenge and the next one introduce students to the concepts of "need" and "want." These lessons are foundational to the subsequent exploration of school rights and responsibilities, but may be unnecessary if students already possess some understanding of what makes something a need. Students begin by examining functional objects (e.g., a lamp, mechanical pencil) to distinguish what these objects require in order to work (i.e., to fulfill their basic function) from what may be nice for them to have, but are not necessary for their operation. Next, students identify those parts of a bicycle that are needed and those that are merely desirable. Finally, students apply their understanding of these concepts by determining the "needed" and "nice to have" parts of a car.

 My favourite activity

3 sessions

This challenge extends students' understanding of "needs" and "wants," previously developed in the context of functional objects, to the more abstract notion of what is needed and wanted for an activity to be carried out safely. Students are presented with numerous useful items on a trip to a local swimming pool or beach. They are asked to determine which items are needed to undertake this activity safely and which items are merely nice to have. Students fill a backpack with the "needed" items and each is given an opportunity to add items they choose. Students then select a fun activity, possibly a planned field trip, and identify potentially useful equipment. Individually or in pairs, students draw a picture of the fun activity and pictures of two "needed" and two "nice to have" items.

Connecting rights with needs

 What is fair to expect?

2 sessions

In this challenge, students are introduced to the concept of a right as something that is fair to expect. Students begin by distinguishing what would and would not be fair to expect of objects (e.g., that lamps will fly, that cars will talk). This notion is extended to what we have a right to expect of people by exploring common expectations in familiar settings, for example at school or in a toy store. Finally, students are asked to draw one thing it would be fair to expect and one thing that would not be fair to expect when visiting a friend's home.

 What I really need

3 sessions

In this challenge, students focus on the needs and wants of people in the context of the rights to a healthy, happy and safe life. Students are introduced to people's needs by listening to a recording of "All I Really Need" by Raffi. This song is the starting point for creating an on-going list of the range of needs that people have a right to expect will be met. Students learn about the needs related to the rights to safety, health and happiness by sorting them into these categories. Finally, students distinguish needs and wants by judging whether the suggested needs are really needed.

 Important learning needs

3 sessions

In the previous challenge, students identified what people need in order to enjoy a happy, healthy and safe life. This two-part challenge focusses on students' needs at school in order to learn. To begin, students recall their own early school experiences and listen to the experiences described in *Franklin Goes to School* by Paulette Bourgeois. From these experiences, students develop a list of needs associated with the right to learn. In the first critical challenge, students sort needs at school according to their importance. In the second challenge, students decide upon, and draw a picture of, the need that is most important for successful learning.

Identifying who is responsible

Who should help us?

5 sessions

This challenge introduces the idea that people have responsibilities to ensure that the needs of others are met. The story, *Franklin's New Friend* by Paulette Bourgeois, provides an opportunity to examine who has responsibilities to help a new student meet his needs. Students explore the thoughts and feelings of characters in the story to appreciate what it is like to be in need and to help someone in need. Then students discuss who has a responsibility to help by considering which characters in the story are both able and expected to help. Students are then introduced to the names and roles of people in the school. Then they are challenged to consider, when given a need, who within the school has a responsibility to help meet this need.

Meeting our needs

4 sessions

This challenge broadens students' understanding of the roles and responsibilities in their school. From interviews conducted with school personnel, students learn that people in various school roles are responsible for helping meet their diverse needs. After examining the responsibilities of an assigned role, students select four important responsibilities and decide which of these responsibilities is the most important in terms of students' needs. Finally, students send a note of appreciation to each person interviewed, acknowledging their help and expressing special thanks for carrying out the most important responsibility attached to their role.

Guess who?

2 sessions

In this challenge, students extend their knowledge of the responsibilities attached to different roles in their school by creating and solving riddles about each role. Students are introduced to a technique for solving riddles and to a four-part structure for developing riddles. Students exchange their completed interview information from the previous challenge with other students who then develop a riddle based on the most important responsibilities attached to the role. After learning about "reasonable guesses," students try to solve the riddles presented to them.

How responsible am I?

5 sessions

In this challenge, students move from examining the responsibilities that others have to help them, to their own responsibilities to help themselves and others. A Shel Silverstein poem explores the consequences when someone does not carry out their responsibilities. Students also consider that their responsibilities include a responsibility to help themselves meet their needs. Using previously developed lists of important needs at school, students select two important responsibilities—one involving a responsibility to themselves and another a responsibility to others. Students clarify what these responsibilities require and then look to see how well they carry out these responsibilities. Based on evidence collected, students assess how responsible they are and what they might do to increase their level of personal responsibility.

In addition to the materials provided in this volume, the supplementary resources listed below are also recommended. The following symbols identify the role of these resources in completing each critical challenge:

N   **Necessary**   The identified resource is necessary to complete the critical challenge as planned.

O   **Options**   The identified resource or one of the other options identified is necessary to complete the critical challenge as planned.

U   **Useful**   The identified resource is helpful, but not necessary, in completing the critical challenge as planned.

		Title	Description	Bibliographic information
4	U	"All I Really Need" (song)	**CD:** *Baby Beluga*	Raffi (1980) Troubadour. (ISBN 1896943-1)
5	N	*Franklin Goes to School*	**Picture book:** This book describes Franklin's first day of school. He is nervous! He worries when he wakes up, all the way to school on the bus and when he steps into his new classroom. Happily, he finds a friendly teacher and other students who help him see and learn new things.	Bourgeois, Paulette (1995) Kids Can Press. (Toronto) (ISBN 1-55074-363-5)
6	N	*Franklin's New Friend*	**Picture book:** A family of moose move into Franklin's neighbourhood. The next day, Moose appears at school and Franklin is assigned the task of being his buddy and helping him find his way around the school.	Bourgeois, Paulette (1997) Kids Can Press. (Toronto) (ISBN 1-55074-363-5)
	U	*Tomorrow's Classroom Today*	**Teacher reference book**	Brownlie, Faye. et al. (1990) Pembroke. (ISBN 0-921217-50-1)
9	N	*Where the Sidewalk Ends: The Poems and Drawings of Shel Silverstein*	**Poem:** "Sarah Cynthia Sylvia Stout Would not Take the Garbage Out" describes the consequences when a young girl does not fulfill her responsibilities at home.	Silverstein, Shel (1974) Harper & Row (New York) (ISBN 06-025667-2)

An important goal of the critical challenge approach is to embed critical thinking into the teaching of the curriculum. The chart below identifies the learning outcomes prescribed in the British Columbia *Integrated Resource Packages* addressed by each critical challenge. For connections with curriculum documents in other provinces look for the title of this publication on the *TC²* website (www.tc2.ca). The following symbols describe the extent to which each learning outcome is satisfied:

X **Fully met** Completing the critical challenge would fully satisfy the prescribed learning outcome.

/ **Partially met** Completing the critical challenge would partially satisfy the prescribed learning outcome.

Grade K/1 Outcomes

Code	Emotional and social development	Code	Intellectual development	Code	Social responsibility
1 2 3 4 5 6 7 8 9	X Listen actively, providing verbal and non-verbal responses appropriate to their stages of development and to their cultures (English Language Arts) / Demonstrate a willingness to present relevant ideas in discussions (English Language Arts) / Draw simple interpretations from personal experiences, oral sources, and visual representation (Social Studies)	1 2 3 4 5	/ Sort information, including ideas, details, and events obtained from a variety of sources (English Language Arts) / Recognize when a problem exists (Personal Planning)	1 2 3 4 5	X Describe the difference between individual needs and wants (Social Studies)
2 5	/ Demonstrate readiness to make choices (Personal Planning)	2 3 4 5 6 9	/ Identify and clarify a problem or issue (Social Studies)	4 5	/ Identify components of a safe and healthy school (Personal Planning)
9	/ Relate consequences to actions and decisions (Personal Planning)			5 6 7 8 9	/ Describe their roles, rights, and responsibilities in school (Social Studies) / Describe the purpose and functions of schools (Social Studies)

Objects have needs

Critical Challenge

Critical question   What does a car need to drive?

Overview   This challenge and the next one introduce students to the concepts of "need" and "want." These lessons are foundational to the subsequent exploration of school rights and responsibilities, but may be unnecessary if students already pose some understanding of what makes something a need. Students begin by examining functional objects (e.g., a lamp, mechanical pencil) to distinguish what these objects require in order to work (i.e., to fulfill their basic function) from what may be nice for them to have, but are not necessary for their operation. Next, students identify those parts of a bicycle that are needed and those that are merely desirable. Finally, students apply their understanding of these concepts by determining the "needed" and "nice to have" parts of a car.

Objectives

Broad understanding   Some parts of an object or a machine are essential to make it work properly; other parts may be nice to have, but they are not necessary to its functioning.

Requisite tools

Background knowledge
- knowledge of the basic features of a bicycle and a car

Criteria for judgment
- criteria for needed parts (e.g., must be present for something to work properly)
- criteria for desirable parts (e.g., adds enjoyment, not necessary for something to work)

Critical thinking vocabulary

Thinking strategies
- sorting
- sentence frame

Habits of mind
- attention to detail

Suggested Activities

Gather selection of working items

➤ Prior to starting the challenge, assemble four or five common functional objects each having two removable parts: one that is an essential working part (e.g., a mechanical pencil without the lead, a pet cage without a door, a lamp not plugged in, an aquarium without water) and another that is a non-essential part (e.g., a clip holder on the mechanical pencil, a shade on the lamp, an exercise wheel in the cage, an ornament in the aquarium).

Session One   *Blackline Master #1*

Explore needed parts

➤ Introduce the idea of "needs" by holding up one of the assembled objects *with the essential part removed* but close at hand. Ask the class what is the object's function or purpose. Try out the object without success (e.g., try to write with the pencil). When it does not work, ask what the object *needs* in order for it to work properly (e.g., a pencil needs lead). When the correct answer has been offered, emphasize the connection between need and proper functioning by asking the question outlined below and inviting individual students to respond using the suggested frame:

criteria for needed part

sentence frame

Q. Does a ___(pencil)___ need ___(lead)___ to ___(write)___ ?
              object   *essential part*   *function*

A. Yes, a ___(pencil)___ needs ___(lead)___ because you can't
                object   *essential part*

    ___(write)___ without it.
       function

Repeat the procedure with each assembled object, using the sentence frame to reinforce the connection between need and proper functioning. After all the needed parts of the objects have been demonstrated, ask students if they can explain what it means for an object to need something in order to function (i.e., "It won't work without it").

Introduce concept of "want"

➤ Use the same objects to introduce the concept of "want." (For this initial lesson, you may prefer to avoid the actual term "want" but instead refer to "nice to have.") Bring each object to a functional state (e.g., add lead to the pencil, plug in the lamp). Point to a non-essential removable part of one of the objects, for example, the clip holder on the pencil, and ask if this part is needed to make the pencil write or is it something that is nice to have but not needed. Invite students to indicate their answer then take off the non-essential part and use the object. Reinforce the point by asking students to respond to the following question using the suggested frame:

criteria for desirable part

Q. Does a___(pencil)___ need___(clip-holder)___ to___(write)___?
          object   *essential part*   *function*

A. No, it is nice to have a___(clip-holder)___ but a___(pencil)___
                             object   *essential part*

does not need it because you can still___(write)___without it.
                                 function

Repeat the procedure with each of the assembled objects, demonstrating the relation between non-essential features and the continued ability to function. Encourage students to use the response frame in each case. Conclude by asking if students can explain what it means that something is "nice to have" (e.g., "the object will work even if this part is missing").

Confirm understanding of concepts

➤ Confirm students' understanding of the concepts of "need" and "want" (nice to have) by inviting them to answer the questions on *What is needed?* (Blackline Master #1). You may carry out this task orally with the entire class by reading a question and the two possible answers, and then inviting students to indicate the correct answer with a "thumbs up" and the incorrect answer with a "thumbs down." If you are concerned that students will not answer on their own, ask them to close their eyes while responding. Alternatively, provide each student with a copy of Blackline Master #1. As an example, read the first sentence and the two possible answers. Ask students to circle either "YES" or "NO" to indicate the correct answer. Discuss the answers they circled and their reasons. Once students understand the task, read each question and pair of possible answers in turn, asking students to circle "YES" or "NO". If some students are not able to work independently with the sheet, scribe their responses.

attention to detail

knowledge of a bicycle

Examine actual bicycles

➤ Take the class to a bicycle stand on the school ground or bring two bicycles into the classroom. Ask the class, "What is a bike supposed to be able to do?" (i.e., ride, take a person from one place to another). Point out, or ask students to indicate, particular parts on the bicycles. Remind students of the previous day's lesson on "needs" and ask the question "What does a bike need in order to for us to ride it?" (e.g., wheels, pedal, handlebars, chain). Mentally note the parts they identify as necessary and ask them to check whether these parts are found on either bike. Then, ask what other things students notice on the bikes that they would like to have, but are not necessary for it to ride (e.g., decorations, bells, drink holders). Mentally note these non-essential parts. If you went outside, return to the classroom.

Identify bicycle parts in picture

➤ Post an enlarged copy (11 x 17) of *Bicycle* (Blackline Master #2) on the board or chart stand. In addition, distribute one copy of *Parts of a bicycle* (Blackline Master #3) to each pair of students. On the enlarged picture, point to a part of the bicycle that is found in the cards on the bottom of Blackline Master #3. Ask students to find the part you have indicated on the small picture of a bike at the top of their sheet. Then, ask students to name the part and to find it in the bike part cards on the bottom of their sheet. To encourage students to think about each part's role in meeting the bike's function, ask "Does a bike need _____ to ride?" (If necessary, prompt with "Would a bike ride without this part?")

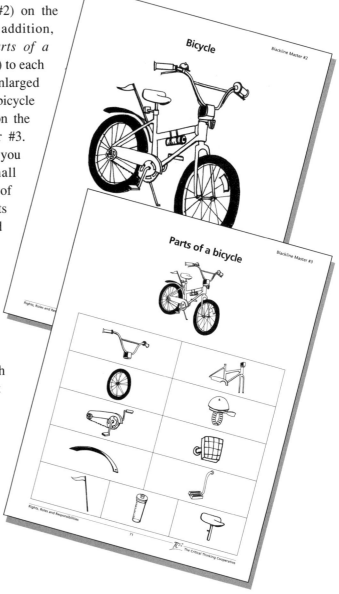

Sort bicycle parts

➤ Once the class has reviewed the bicycle parts and responded to the questions, ask each pair of students to cut out the cards found on Blackline Master #3. Then, recalling the discussion of what a bicycle needs to work, ask students to sort the cards into two piles: "Needed" and "Nice to have." Use any disagreements to clarify what makes a part needed (i.e., must be present to ride). When the cards are sorted, provide each pair of students with an enlarged copy (11 x 17) of *Needed or nice?* (Blackline Master #4). Ask students to paste their sorted cards in the appropriate column of their chart.

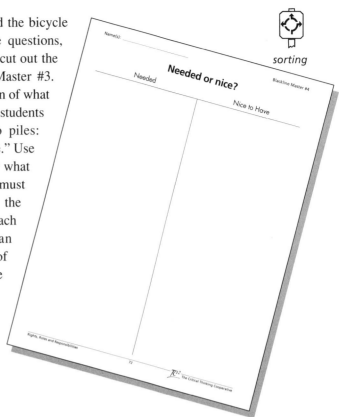

Draw and identify parts

➤ OPTIONAL: After each pair of students has completed its chart, check students' understanding by asking *each* student to draw a picture of a bike they would like to have. Encourage students to print or dictate to you sentences indicating whether various parts they have drawn are needed or nice to have. Ask students to use the appropriate sentence frame for each part:

A bike needs a _____ because you cannot ride without it.

It's nice to have a _____ but a bike does not need it because you can still ride without it.

Introduce car parts

➤ When students are able to respond using the sentence frames, invite the class to apply what it learned about needs to distinguish various parts of a car. Provide each student with a copy of *Parts of a car* (Blackline Master #5). Post an enlarged copy (11 x 17) of *Car* (Blackline Master #6) on the board or chart stand. On the enlarged picture, point to a part of the car that is found in the cards on the bottom of Blackline Master #5. Ask students to find the part you have indicated on the small picture of a car at the top of their sheet. Review each part and ask students to name the part and identify its function. If students are not familiar with these parts, take them to examine an actual car in the parking lot and ask them to point out the parts and to suggest their purposes.

knowledge of a car

Car
Blackline Master #6

Parts of a car
Blackline Master #5

Present the critical challenge

➤ When students have identified all the car parts on their cards and know their functions, remind them how they looked at the parts of a bicycle to decide what was needed and what was nice to have. Invite students to do the same with a car by posing the critical question:

What does a car need to drive?

Distribute an enlarged copy (11 x 17) of Blackline Master #4 to each student. Ask them to cut out their cards, sort the parts into "needs" and "nice to have" piles and then paste them on Blackline Master #4 as they had done for the bicycle.

➤ OPTIONAL: Ask students to complete each sentence frame on *Driving a car* (Blackline Master #7) either by drawing pictures, printing the words or dictating to you. If desired, give students sufficient copies of Blackline Master #7 to complete a frame for each identified part of the car.

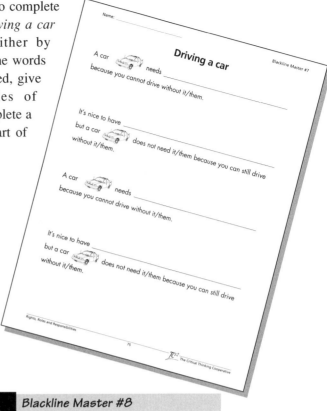

Evaluation   *Blackline Master #8*

➤ Assess students' understanding of the needed and wanted parts of an object using the rubric *Assessing needs and wants* (Blackline Master #8). The sources of evidence and criteria for this assessment are listed below:

- use students' responses to the class discussion on the needed parts of various objects and their answers on *What is needed?* (Blackline Master #1) to assess their ability to identify something that is needed for an object to function;

- use students' responses pasted on *Needed or nice?* (Blackline Master #4) and recorded on *Driving a car* (Blackline Master #7) to assess their ability to distinguish needs and wants.

Reaching the "basic understanding" level on the rubric may be appropriate for many early primary students.

Explore other objects' needs

➤ As a science extension, guide students in exploring the needs of other functional objects in their classroom, home or community. For example, students might learn from books or field visits what school furnaces or fire engines need in order to work.

My favourite activity

Critical Challenge

Critical task Draw two things you need and two things that would be nice to have for a fun activity.

Overview This challenge extends students' understanding of "needs" and "wants," previously developed in the context of functional objects, to the more abstract notion of what is needed and wanted for an activity to be carried out safely. Students are presented with numerous useful items on a trip to a local swimming pool or beach. They are asked to determine which items are needed to undertake this activity safely and which items are merely nice to have. Students fill a backpack with the "needed" items and each is given an opportunity to add items they choose. Students then select a fun activity, possibly a planned field trip, and identify potentially useful equipment. Individually or in pairs, students draw a picture of the fun activity and pictures of two "needed" and two "nice to have" items.

Objectives

Broad understanding Some things are necessary in order to participate in an activity; other things may be nice to have, but they are not necessary to participate safely.

Requisite tools *Background knowledge*
- knowledge of swimming
- knowledge of fun activity

Criteria for judgment
- criteria for needed equipment (e.g., must be present to participate safely in the activity)
- criteria for desirable equipment (e.g., adds enjoyment, not necessary for participation in the activity)

Critical thinking vocabulary

Thinking strategies
- brainstorming
- sorting
- sentence frame

Habits of mind

Suggested Activities

Pre-planning

➤ Gather ten or more items that a child would need and might want when swimming at a local pool or beach (e.g., bathing suit, towel, plastic bag for wet suit, snack, admission money, locker money, water wings, inflatable ball, paddle board, snorkel tube). Collect a few small boxes of varying sizes (e.g., jewelery box, shoe box) that can be used to simulate objects that students might suggest for swimming that you had not brought along. Paste a piece of paper on the top of these boxes to allow you to sketch any object that students might suggest. In Session One, bring the assembled items in a large box along with a backpack that is an appropriate size for students. You should have more items than could possibly fit into the backpack.

Session One

Identify possible items

➤ Invite students to imagine they are going swimming to a local pool (or beach) and that each student must decide what to take along. Ask the class to suggest items that might be useful. Invite students to brainstorm items used when swimming. If students are unfamiliar with brainstorming, explain that it is a strategy for generating lots of ideas. Encourage students to share any ideas they can think of. You may want to model this by suggesting a few items (e.g., "Perhaps we could bring….") As students identify items you have assembled, pull them out of the box and place them on the carpet. If students identify an item you do not have, quickly sketch and label the object on one of the small boxes and add it to the collection. When brainstorming, all suggestions are accepted, even those that do not seem relevant. If students do not mention all the items you have assembled, lift the items from the large box and ask if they might be useful, before adding them to the collection on the carpet.

knowledge of swimming

brainstorming

Review needs and wants

➤ Draw attention to the collection of items on the carpet and bring out the backpack. Suggest that each student should have to carry the items he or she decides to bring in a backpack like the one you have brought to class. Invite opinions as to whether or not all the items will fit into the backpack. If any students are uncertain, demonstrate by trying (unsuccessfully) to pack the items. Discuss as a class how students might decide which items to bring and which to leave behind. Encourage students to see the value of starting with the items that they would need for the activity and then, if there is room, proceeding with items that might be nice to have. Remind students how they decided what a bicycle and a car needed and suggest that they start by considering what they must have if they are to swim in a safe manner. Reinforce what makes something a need—in this case, what is required in order to participate safely in the activity (e.g., Could students swim and do so safely without it?). Reinforce the concept of "want" as items that would be nice to have but are not essential to the activity.

criteria for need and want

Demonstrate sorting

➤ To assist the class in sorting the items, place two hoops on the carpet near the collected items. Label the hoops "needed" and "nice to have." Focus students' attention on the "needed" hoop. Invite a student to select one item from the collection that would be needed for swimming and place the item in the "needed" hoop, giving a reason why it is needed. Next, focus students' attention on the "nice to have" hoop. Invite a student to select one item that would be nice to have, and place it in the "nice to have" hoop, giving a reason why it is not needed. You may want to use the following sentence frames to pose questions and structure students' responses:

Q. Do we need a ___(bathing suit)___ to ___(swim safely)___ ?
                      item   *activity*

A. We need a ___(bathing suit)___ because we can't ___(swim safely)___
             essential item   *activity*

   without it.

A. It is nice to have a ___(beach ball)___ but we do not need it
                 non-essential item

   because we can still ___(swim safely)___ without it.
                     activity

Sort needs and wants

➤ Once the two students have demonstrated the task, organize the sorting of the other items, either by you selecting items or by student volunteers selecting items from the collection. In either case, a volunteer is to place each item in one of the hoops and explain why. You may want to use the sentence frames outlined above. If a student thinks that an item is neither needed nor nice to have, ask the student to place it back in the large box. When all the items have been sorted, ask students to look carefully at the contents of the two hoops. Solicit any questions or suggestions for moving items from one hoop to the other. Remind students that the items selected as needs must be brought along to allow them to swim safely and the "nice to have" items are not necessary. Keep separate the items in the two hoops for use in the next session.

Session Two

Pack the "needed" items

➤ Bring out the two sorted piles of items and the backpack. Ask the class which pile should be packed first. When they agree that the "needed" pile should be the priority, invite a student to pack the backpack with all these items. If all the needed items will not fit into the backpack, help the class see that some items are least needed or perhaps merely "nice to have." It is more likely that there will be additional room in the backpack, so students can now consider items in the "nice to have" hoop that they would choose to bring.

Select "nice to have" items

➤ Point out that the "needed" hoop contained the commonly agreed-upon items required for safe swimming. When choosing from the "nice to have" hoop, each student may have different wants. Hand one student the backpack containing the "needed" items and ask the student to select items from the "nice to have" pile. Allow the student to place as many items in the backpack as will fit, all the while giving reasons why they would be nice to have. When the student has completed his or her selection, empty only the "nice to have" items from the backpack, returning them to their pile. Invite a few more students to make their selections, following the procedure just outlined. After these students have filled the backpack with "nice to have" items, ask the class to notice if students selected different items.

Allow everyone to fill the backpack

➤ To allow every student an opportunity to pack the backpack without requiring the entire class to watch each turn, move the equipment to a corner of the room. Organize students in pairs to visit the site when their names are called or when they have completed assigned tasks. You will need to check that all the "nice to have" items are removed after each packing.

Session Three
Blackline Master #9

Select a fun activity

➤ When all students have had the opportunity to pack the backpack, invite them to consider the needs and wants related to another activity. Depending upon students' ability to work independently, the activity could be one for the entire class, or each student might think of a favourite activity. Alternatively, if you are planning an field trip with your students, use this event as the focus for the challenge. Announce to students that they are going to decide on the equipment to bring when taking part in a fun activity. Assist students in identifying appropriate activities, ranging from sports (e.g., soccer, baseball) to other recreational activities (e.g., hiking, picnicking in the park). Create a list of possible activities and illustrate with stick drawings. Decide on one activity for the entire class, or invite each student (or pair of students) to select a favourite activity. Steer students towards activities that involve several pieces of equipment so as to require that students choose between needed and wanted items.

Identify possible equipment

➤ Once the activity (or activities) has been selected, ask students to suggest at least four pieces of equipment that would be useful for each activity under consideration. List the equipment in words and in stick drawings next to the activity, as suggested below. If the class is considering a common activity, bring in actual equipment to make the activity more real for students.

knowledge of fun activity

Fun activity	Equipment
Hiking	water bottle
	first aid kit
	hat
	walking stick

Present the challenge

➤ OPTIONAL: Ask students to complete each sentence frame on *Driving a car* (Blackline Master #7) either by drawing pictures, printing the words or dictating to you. If desired, give students sufficient copies of Blackline Master #7 to complete a frame for each identified part of the car.

Draw and identify parts

➤ When an equipment list for each activity has been created, distribute an enlarged copy (11 x 17) of *Planning for an activity* (Blackline Master #9) to each student (or pair of students). Ask students to draw a picture showing themselves engaged in the fun activity in the top portion of the sheet. When this is complete, present the critical task:

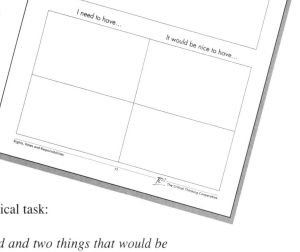

Draw two things you need and two things that would be nice to have for your fun activity.

In the four squares in the bottom half of Blackline Master #9, ask students to draw two pictures of what they would need to participate safely and two items they would want, but do not need for the activity. Remind students to consult the chart for ideas about the equipment related to their fun activity. If students are able, encourage them to print the name of the activity and each piece of equipment on the lines provided; other students can have these names scribed for them.

Evaluation   *Blackline Master #8*

Assess needs and wants

➤ Assess students' understanding of needed and wanted equipment for their fun activity using the rubric *Assessing needs and wants* (Blackline Master #8). The sources of evidence for this assessment are students' responses when sorting swimming items and their answers on *Planning for an activity* (Blackline Master #9). Reaching the "basic understanding" level on the rubric may be appropriate for many early primary students.

What is fair to expect?

Critical Challenge

Critical task
Draw pictures of one thing it is fair to expect and one thing it is not fair to expect when you visit a friend's home.

Overview
In this challenge, students are introduced to the concept of a right as something that is fair to expect. Students begin by distinguishing what would and would not be fair to expect of objects (e.g., that lamps will fly, that cars will talk). This notion is extended to what we have a right to expect of people by exploring common expectations in familiar settings, for example at school or in a toy store. Finally, students are asked to draw one thing it would be fair to expect and one thing that would not be fair to expect when visiting a friend's home.

Objectives

Broad understanding
We have a right to expect certain things and no right to expect other things.

Requisite tools

Background knowledge
- knowledge of the performance of familiar objects
- knowledge of people's behaviour in common settings

Criteria for judgment
- criteria for a fair expectation (e.g., something that should occur)

Critical thinking vocabulary

Thinking strategies

Habits of mind

Suggested Activities

Review understanding of needs

➤ Hold up three functional objects found in the classroom (e.g., pencil, book, ruler) and announce to the class that you have recently purchased these items, but you are disappointed because they do not work in the ways you expected, for example, the lamp doesn't fly, the pencil doesn't talk and the ruler doesn't give hugs. Ask the class if they think you should return the objects to the store. Use their answers to introduce the notion of what is "fair to expect" (e.g., Is it fair for me to expect that a pencil will talk?) as something that "should happen" or that "we have a right to expect." If students suggest that so-called "unreasonable" expectations do occur (for example, pencils can fly in the movies and in fictional books), stress that although this may happen in special cases, your concern is whether or not it is fair to expect this to occur in real life with objects they see in the classroom.

Record "fair expectations" for objects

➤ Explain to the class that you need their help in deciding what is and is not fair for you to expect. Select an object (e.g., the pencil) and suggest several possibilities including one reasonable expectation (e.g., Is it fair to expect a pencil to fly? To sing? To write?). Create a chart on the board or on paper, titled "Is it fair to expect…." Create three columns: one for the object and a column each for yes and no answers. Record student responses in words and stick drawings as suggested below. Add to the chart by suggesting both fair and unreasonable expectations for other objects. Throughout the process, interchange the phrases "Is it fair to expect…" and "Do I have a right to expect…." Leave space on the chart to add other items in a later session.

knowledge of familiar objects

Is it fair to expect…

	Yes	No
pencil	write	talk fly
book	tell a story	give hugs
lamp	give light	fly sing

➤ Confirm students' understanding of what is fair to expect (have a right to expect) by inviting them to answer the questions on *What is fair to expect?* (Blackline Master #10). This assessment can be done orally by reading a question and then inviting students to indicate the correct answer with a "thumbs up" and the incorrect answer with a "thumbs down." If you are concerned that students will not answer on their own, ask them to close their eyes while responding. Alternatively, provide each student with a copy of Blackline Master #10. As an example, read the first question and ask students to circle either "YES" or "NO" to indicate whether it is fair to expect that a pencil will fly. Discuss the answers they circled and their reasons. Once students understand the task, read the remaining questions in turn, inviting students to circle the correct answer—"YES" or "NO". If some students are unable to work independently with the sheet, record their responses for them.

criteria for fair expectation

Name:

What is fair to expect?

Blackline Master #10

Is it fair to expect that...

a pencil will fly

a lamp will give light — YES — NO

a knife will sing — YES — NO

— YES — NO

Do I have a right to expect...

a pencil will swim

a lamp will sing — YES — NO

a knife will cut — YES — NO

— YES — NO

Rights, Roles and Responsibilities

78

Session Two   *Blackline Master #11*

➤ Draw students' attention to the "Is it fair to expect…" chart created in the previous session. Refresh students' memory of the concept by suggesting a functional object not already on the list (e.g., radio) and by inviting students to indicate what might be fair to expect (e.g., that it can play music) and might not be fair to expect (e.g., that it can fly).

➤ Suggest to students that it is fair to expect things of people, not just of objects. Ask students to indicate which of the following are examples of fair and of unfair expectations of people:

knowledge of people's behaviour

• If I give someone a present, is it fair to expect that the person will thank me? That the person will give me a million dollars? That the person will give me five presents in return?

• When I go to school is it fair to expect that my teacher will help me learn? That the teacher will let me do anything I want? That I will have a place to sit?

• If I go to the toy store is it fair to expect that there will be toys for me to buy? That they will let me break every toy in the store? That they will give me any toy I want for free? That they will let me look around the store if I am careful?

Record students' answers in the appropriate columns on the "Is it fair to expect..." chart, using a simple (and perhaps humorous) stick drawing to illustrate each idea. As was previously suggested, interchange the phrases "Is it fair to expect..." and "Do I have a right to expect...."

Present the critical task

➤ When it is apparent that students can extend the notion of fair expectations to people's behaviour, distribute an enlarged copy (11 x 17) of *Visiting my friend's home* (Blackline Master #11) to each student. Ask each student to draw in the top box a picture of the student playing with his or her friend at the friend's home. When this is complete, present the critical task:

> *Draw pictures of one thing it is fair to expect and one thing it is not fair to expect when you visit a friend's home.*

Explain that students are to think of something they have a right to expect when visiting their friend's home. They should draw a picture of this in the box on the bottom left. In the box on the bottom right, students are to draw a picture of something they do not have a right to expect when visiting their friend's home. For those students who are unable to think of what to draw, suggest a fair and an unfair expectation and allow them to decide in which box each expectation belongs. Possible suggestions are "be allowed to break all the furniture" and "be treated nicely." As students finish their drawings, help them print, or scribe for them, a sentence at the bottom of each box explaining the actions in each picture.

Assess right to expect

➤ Assess students' understanding of fair and unfair expectations using the rubric *Assessing fair expectations* (Blackline Master #12). The sources of evidence are students' contributions to the "What is fair to expect…" chart, and their answers on *What is fair to expect?* (Blackline Master #10) and on *Visiting my friend's home* (Blackline Master #11). Reaching the "basic understanding" level on the rubric may be appropriate for many early primary students.

What I really need

Critical Challenge

Critical task Decide if you really need these things to be happy, healthy or safe.

Overview In this challenge, students focus on the needs and wants of people in the context of the rights to a healthy, happy and safe life. Students are introduced to people's needs by listening to a recording of "All I Really Need" by Raffi. This song is the starting point for creating an on-going list of the range of needs that people have a right to expect will be met. Students learn about the needs related to the rights to safety, health and happiness by sorting them into these categories. Finally, students distinguish needs and wants by judging whether the suggested needs are really needed.

Objectives

Broad understanding People have a right to expect that basic needs for a safe, healthy and happy life will be met.

Requisite tools

Background knowledge
- knowledge of people's needs for safety, health and happiness

Criteria for judgment
- criteria for people's basic needs (e.g., must be present to be healthy, safe or happy)
- criteria for people's wants (e.g., adds enjoyment, something that is desired but can live happily, safely and healthfully without them)

Critical thinking vocabulary

Thinking strategies
- sorting
- sentence frame

Habits of mind

Suggested Activities

Pre-planning

➤ We propose using Raffi's song, "All I Really Need," to explore what people need in order to be healthy, safe and happy. In his song, Raffi explains that his greatest need is the love of his family. This love makes him feel happy and safe. If you are unable to locate this song (see References), find another song or a picture book that deals with people's basic needs.

Session One

Review needs

➤ The first two challenges in this unit focussed on the differences between what is needed and what is nice to have in the contexts of functioning objects and safe participation in activities. If your students already understood these concepts, you may not have made use of these challenges. To introduce the current lesson on people's needs, ask students to recall what they learned about (or simply to imagine) what happens when something that is needed is missing. As suggested in the chart below, identify a few functional objects (e.g., lamp, bicycle, car) and ask students what happens when things that these objects need in order to work are missing (e.g., lamps will not give light). Record students' answers in a stick drawing and in words. Then ask students to identify things needed for each of these objects to work properly. Repeat the same procedure with participation in a few activities (e.g., swimming, skating, skipping).

When needs are not met

	What happens when needs are NOT met?	Things that are needed	
lamp	won't light	electricity	light bulb
bike	won't ride	wheels	pedals
swimming	can't swim might drown	bathing suit	life jacket
skating	can't skate	ice	skates

➤ Now ask students what happens to people when they do not get what they need. Prompt students with questions such as "What would happen to us if we didn't have food? doctors? friends?" Record their answers in the middle column of the chart as suggested below. Remind students of the fair expectations they have for objects. Ask students if it is fair to expect that a lamp will light or that a bike will ride. Extend this notion to people by comparing a lamp that does light up to a person who is sad—neither can function or live as they should. Help students recognize three aspects of basic well-being or human functioning that people have a right to expect. These are expectations of being safe, healthy and happy. Ask students to suggest a few things that people need to be happy, safe and healthy. Record these in the third column of the chart.

	What happens when needs are NOT met?	**Things that are needed**
people	be sad/cry	friends
	get sick/die	food
	get hurt	doctors

➤ Announce that the class is about to listen to a song describing one person's needs in order to be happy and safe. Play Raffi's song, "All I Really Need" and ask students the following questions:

- What is important to Raffi in this song? What does he need? (e.g., love of his family)

- Why is this an important need? How does it help him? (e.g., makes him happy, feel safe)

On the above chart, record any additional needs identified by students.

*knowledge of
people's needs*

Reinforce understanding of rights

➤ Enlarge to ledger size (11 x 17) a copy of *Rights graphics* Blackline Master #13A–B) and cut out each graphic. Paste the first three—the rights to be safe, healthy and happy—on separate pieces of chart paper for students to examine. Save the fourth graphic—a right to learn—for use in a later challenge. To begin, ask students if they know what being safe, healthy and happy means. Invite students to explain what each looks like and sounds like (e.g., strong, not hurt, not sick, not crying, smiling, laughing, feeling good). Record these words around the appropriate graphic. Help students see why these rights are so important by discussing what it feels like when we are not safe, healthy or happy. Because of their importance, everyone has a right to expect that these will happen, just as we have a right to expect our new pencil will write. Review with students what it means to say we have a right. Remind students that a right means that something should happen.

Connect needs to rights

➤ Underneath each right, print the phrase "We need…" Remind students that just as a bicycle needs wheels to work properly, people have needs to be healthy, safe and happy. Invite students to suggest what each of us needs in order to be safe. Using a large index card for each suggestion, record student ideas in stick drawings and words. Attach these to the paper under the "We need…" heading. Do the same for the other two rights. If a need applies to more than one right, create more than one index card. Prompt students by drawing attention to the chart from the previous lesson that shows Raffi's needs. Copy any needs from that chart onto index cards and attach them under the appropriate right. After students have exhausted their suggestions, offer additional examples of needs and invite students to identify the corresponding right(s). You may want to suggest such needs as stop signs, medicine, exercise, water, holding a parent's hand to cross the street, warm clothing. Record these suggestions on separate cards and ask students to attach them under the appropriate right.

Reinforce understanding

➤ To reinforce students' understanding of the corresponding needs for each basic right, take down a handful of the index cards from the three charts and invite students to re-attach the cards onto the appropriate sheet of paper. You may want to pose the following question as you hand each index card to a student:

sorting

> *Q.   Do we need _____(friends)_____ to be happy, or to be healthy or to be safe?*

If you want many students to work on this activity concurrently, photocopy several sets of index cards and additional copies of the graphics found on Master #13A–B. Cut out and distribute a set of cards and the three rights graphics to groups of students, who are to sort the needs according to the applicable rights. After the activity, re-attach the index cards to the three charts for use in subsequent critical challenges.

Distinguish personal needs from wants

➤ Extend students' understanding of needs by reintroducing the notion of nice to have. Select a need from one of the three charts (e.g., we need friends), and ask students what exactly is meant by this statement. Does it mean we need a friend or thousands of friends? Use the following sentence frame to present the issue:

criteria for needs

criteria for wants

> Q. Do we need ____(a friend or thousands of friends)____ to be
> *essential and non-essential condition*
>
> ____(happy)____ ?
> *right*

sentence frame

Direct students to respond to the question using the appropriate sentence frame:

> A. We need ____(a friend)____ because we can't be ____(happy)____
> *essential condition*   *right*
> without one.

> A. It is nice to have ____(thousands of friends)____ but we do not
> *non-essential condition*
> need them because we can still be ____(happy)____ without them.
> *right*

Identify an essential and non-essential condition for several other needs listed on the charts (e.g., a hug each morning or a hug every minute, a stop sign on all busy streets or one on every street). Invite students to respond using the appropriate sentence frame. Use these responses as opportunities to reinforce that needs are what *must* be met if we are to have a safe, healthy and happy life.

➤ OPTIONAL: If students are able to grasp the idea, invite them to discuss exactly how many friends or hugs a person might need to feel safe and happy. Remind them, for example, that they agreed they needed at least one friend, but not thousands. Would one friend be enough or does everyone need at least two friends? Encourage students to share the reasons for their answers.

**Present
the challenge**

➤ Provide each student with a copy of *What I really need* (Blackline Master #14). Present the critical challenge:

Decide if you really need these things to be happy, healthy or safe.

Read each of the questions and the accompanying pairs of possible answers. Ask students to circle either "YES" or "NO" to indicate their answer for each question. If some students are not able to work independently with the sheet, scribe their responses. You may carry out this task orally by reading aloud each question and the two possible answers and then inviting students to indicate correct answers with a "thumbs up" and incorrect answers with a "thumbs down." If you are concerned that students will not answer on their own, ask them to close their eyes while responding.

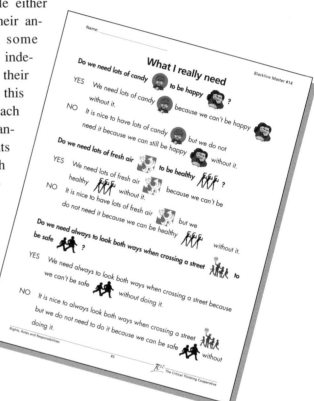

Evaluation　　　　　*Blackline Master #8*

**Assess needs
and wants**

➤ Assess students' understanding of people's needs and wants for different rights using the rubric *Assessing needs and wants* (Blackline Master #8). The sources of evidence and the two criteria for this assessment are listed below:

- use students' responses to the class discussion on the corresponding needs for each right and the sorting of index cards to assess students' ability to relate particular needs to the corresponding right;

- use students' responses to the class activity involving sentence frames and their answers to *What I really need* (Blackline Master #14) to assess their ability to distinguish needs and wants for different rights.

Reaching the "basic understanding" level on the rubric may be appropriate for many early primary students.

References

Raffi (1980). "All I Really Need," *Baby Beluga* CD. Troubadour. (ISBN 1896943-1)

Important learning needs

Critical Challenge

Critical questions

A. Which of these needs are more important and which are less important for your learning?

B. Which need is most important for your learning?

Overview

In the previous challenge, students identified what people need in order to enjoy a happy, healthy and safe life. This two-part challenge focusses on students' needs at school in order to learn. To begin, students recall their own early school experiences and listen to the experiences described in *Franklin Goes to School* by Paulette Bourgeois. From these experiences, students develop a list of needs associated with the right to learn. In the first critical challenge, students sort needs at school according to their importance. In the second challenge, students decide upon, and draw a picture of, the need that is most important for successful learning.

Objectives

Broad understanding

Students have needs that must be met if they are to learn; some of these needs are more important for success in learning than others.

Requisite tools

Background knowledge
- knowledge of school conditions
- knowledge of what students need in order to learn

Criteria for judgment
- criteria for important needs (e.g., greatly affects the results, cannot be met in any other manner)
- criteria for most important need (e.g., is needed most often, would be really missed)

Critical thinking vocabulary

Thinking strategies
- sorting

Habits of mind

Suggested Activities

Obtain a suitable resource

➤ Locate a copy of *Franklin Goes to School* by Paulette Bourgeois. This book describes Franklin's first day of school. He is nervous! He worries all the way to school on the bus and when he steps into his new classroom. Happily, he finds a friendly teacher and other students who help him see that he can do many of the things expected at school and that there is abundant help for learning new things. If you are unable to locate this book (see References), find a substitute resource that deals with students' needs at school.

Session One

Explore students' early school needs

➤ Before reading the book *Franklin Goes to School*, ask students to share stories about their first days at school. As they share these stories, encourage students to indicate what they needed at this time in order to learn and be happy and safe. Remind students that a need is something that they had to have in order to participate in the first days of school. Print on the board "When I first went to school I needed…" and record beneath this title the suggested needs that emerge from students' stories (e.g., to have someone to walk them to school, to show them where to sit, to be their friend).

knowledge of school conditions

Read the story

➤ Explain that you are going to read a story about a boy's first day at school. Ask students to listen carefully to see if this boy's needs were the same as or different than the needs of students in the class. Next to the chart of students' needs, write the title "When Franklin first went to school he needed…." Begin reading the story, *Franklin Goes to School*. You may want to stop after the part where Franklin gets on the bus. At this point, ask students to identify what Franklin needed in order to prepare for school (e.g., pencil, ruler, full tummy, hug, book bag). Read the rest of the book, asking students to identify Franklin's needs when he got to school. Add these needs to the chart. Focus on the things Franklin needed from Mr. Owl (e.g., help with reading, praise for knowing his colours, an invitation to learn new things at school) and on the supplies he needed to complete his work.

Compare needs

➤ After listing Franklin's needs, ask students to compare the two lists: "When I first went to school I needed…" and "When Franklin first went to school he needed…." Invite students to add items from Franklin's list to their list of needs. Save these two lists for use in the next session.

Identify type of needs

➤ Draw attention to the three "rights" charts with the needs listed under each. Remind students that we have at least three types of needs that must be met: needs related to our health, our safety and our happiness. Review a few examples of each type. Now draw attention to the list titled, "When I first went to school I needed…" developed in the previous session. Select a few needs that are concerned with health, safety and happiness, and then identify a need associated with learning. Ask students to suggest why this last item is needed. Draw attention to other needs that students require for learning at school.

Introduce right to learn

➤ Explain that in addition to the three rights (i.e., healthy, safe and happy) discussed thus far, we have another right, one that is specially connected to school— the right to learn. Paste an enlarged graphic of this right found on *Rights graphics* (Blackline Master #13B) on a large sheet of paper next to the other three rights. Invite students to suggest what the right to learn looks like and sounds like (e.g., reading, listening, wondering) and record these words around the graphic. As before, print below the graphic "We need…" and ask students to help you list things that are needed to satisfy this right. Record these suggestions in print and stick drawings on large index cards and attach them to the chart.

Explore importance of needs

➤ Select two cards from the "Meeting our learning needs" chart—one that is clearly very important (e.g., the teacher) and another that is obviously of lesser importance (e.g., a ruler). Invite students to imagine that they cannot have both needs met, that they could only have one or the other. Which one would they choose and why. Ask students to think of what would happen if they did not have a teacher (e.g., no stories, no hugs, no help with printing). What would happen if they had no rulers (e.g., hard to make straight lines, couldn't measure things)? Encourage students to see that having no teacher would make any learning very hard, but they could still learn a lot without a ruler. Select additional pairs of cards, for example, books and book bags or friends and erasers, and ask students to decide which of the pair would be more important to their learning.

criteria for important need

Rights, Roles and Responsibilities   31   *TC²* The Critical Thinking Cooperative

Present the first challenge

➤ Select approximately four pairs of index cards that identify things students need for their learning. Include both essential and non-essential items. Match the paired items so students will not be expected to choose between items of equal importance. Photocopy a set for each pair of students. When photocopying the cards, choose pairings that will advance students' thinking, but not frustrate them. Distribute the sets of four pairs along with an enlarged copy (11 x 17) of *Meeting our needs at school* (Blackline Master #15). Present the critical question:

Which of these needs are more important and which are less important for your learning?

Name(s): _____

Meeting our needs at school   *Blackline Master #15*

Which items are...

MORE important

LESS important

Rights, Roles and Responsibilities

84

The Critical Thinking Cooperative

sorting

With a partner, students should sort the cards into two piles—those needs that are more important and those that are less important to learning. Suggest that students select a pair of joined cards and cut them apart. Working with their partner, they are to decide which card goes in the more important pile and which goes in the less important pile. Encourage students to think of what would happen if they had to do without an item. Which loss would make learning harder? Which do they need more in order to learn? Each pair of students should repeat the process until all pairs of cards are separated and sorted. At this point, students should glue their cards to Blackline Master #15, placing the more important pile on one side and the less important pile on the other. Circulate to see if students are able to offer reasons for their decisions.

Introduce most important need

➤ Ask students to think of the most important person or persons in their life. Invite them to explain what makes this person (these people) so very important. Draw out from students' comments that the person is always doing things for the student and would be really missed. Now turn students' attention to the things they need in order to learn. Ask if some of these things are more important than the rest. Suggest that the most important needs are probably needed often, not just once in a while, and that if the need were not met, it would make a big difference. Walk students through the list of most important needs pasted on their sheet of paper (Blackline Master #15). Help paint a picture for students of how often each of these needs arises and what trying to learn would be like without them.

knowledge of needs

criteria for most important need

Present the second challenge

➤ When students seem to appreciate the implications of these needs for their learning, present the following critical question:

Which need is most important for your learning?

Encourage students to look to the list on Blackline Master #15 and also to the other needs on the larger chart. Ask students to draw a picture on *What I need most so I can learn* (Blackline Master #16) that shows them learning while this need is met. Assist students in completing the sentence at the bottom of their picture. Post their completed drawings in the classroom.

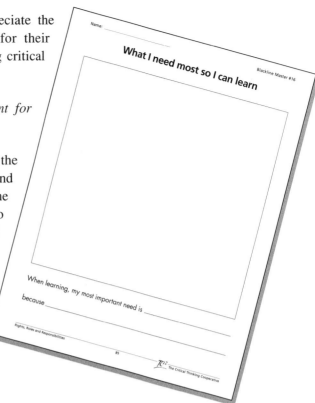

Evaluation   *Blackline Master #17*

Assess important needs

➤ Assess students' understanding of their important needs related to learning using the rubric *Assessing important needs and responsibilities* (Blackline Master #17). The sources of evidence for this assessment are student responses on *Meeting our needs at school* (Blackline Master #15) and *What I need most so I can learn* (Blackline Master #16). Reaching the "basic understanding" level on the rubric may be appropriate for many early primary students.

Resources

Bourgeois, Paulette (1995). *Franklin Goes to School* (illustrated by Brenda Clark). Toronto: Kids Can Press. (ISBN 1-55074-363-5)

Extension

Graph results

➤ Create a graph of students' choices of their most important need.

Who should help us?

Critical Challenge

Critical question   Who has a responsibility to help us meet this need?

Overview   This challenge introduces the idea that people have responsibilities to ensure that the needs of others are met. The story, *Franklin's New Friend* by Paulette Bourgeois, provides an opportunity to examine who has responsibilities to help a new student meet his needs. Students explore the thoughts and feelings of characters in the story to appreciate what it is like to be in need and to help someone in need. Then students discuss who has a responsibility to help by considering which characters in the story are both able and expected to help. Students are then introduced to the names and roles of people in the school. Then they are challenged to consider, when given a need, who within the school has a responsibility to help meet this need.

Objectives

Broad understanding   There are many in the school community who have some responsibility to help students meet their school needs; but these responsibilities depend on the role and the person's ability to help.

Requisite tools   *Background knowledge*
- knowledge of roles and responsibilities in school

Criteria for judgment
- criteria for responsibility (e.g. able to help, expected to help)

Critical thinking vocabulary
- evidence (reasons)

Thinking strategies
- thinking and feeling bubbles

Habits of mind
- empathy

Suggested Activities

Locate a suitable resource

➤ In this challenge, the book *Franklin's New Friend* (see References) is used to help students imagine how others feel and think when they are in need at school. In the story, a family of moose move into Franklin's neighbourhood. The next day, Moose appears at school and Franklin is assigned the task of being his buddy and helping him find his way around school. Our objective in using this story is to help students imagine how people in these kinds of situations feel. This purpose can also be met by using *Second Step Program* picture cards or collections of pictures from books that show typical school situations (e.g., children playing together, a child standing apart from a group, a child being bullied, an injured child being helped).

Prepare materials

➤ Before Session One, prepare a large sheet of drawing paper for each child by folding it in four equal segments. Duplicate multiple copies of *Thinking and feeling bubbles* (Blackline Master #18), and cut out the heart- and cloud-shaped bubbles. Students will use these bubbles to record characters' thoughts and feelings in the Franklin story. In Session Three, students learn about various roles in their school. In preparation, you may want to take photographs of the people who fill these roles in your school for use when introducing each role.

Session One

Introduce feeling and thinking bubbles

➤ Announce to the class that they are about to hear a story about a new student coming to school and how this student was helped by others. Ask if students have ever been in a new situation where they did not know anyone and needed help. Quickly sketch a simple drawing of the scene identified by one of your students. Ask how your student felt and what he or she thought. Introduce the idea, developed by Faye Brownlie (see References), of using feeling bubbles (like cartoon thinking bubbles, but heart-shaped) and thinking bubbles (cloud-shaped) to illustrate how someone feels and what someone is thinking about. To demonstrate the strategy, paste one of the heart-shaped bubbles onto your sketch, pointing to the child's chest, and draw a symbol or print words to describe the

thinking and feeling bubbles

empathy

student's feeling (e.g., afraid). If relevant, ask how other characters in the scene, including someone who helped your student, might have felt. Paste heart-shaped bubbles pointed to their chests and draw or print key words in these bubbles to represent their feelings. Invite students to suggest what the people might be thinking (e.g., "I want to go home!"). Illustrate or print their thoughts in these bubbles, and paste the thinking bubbles above the appropriate characters' heads.

Introduce the story

➤ Begin reading *Franklin's New Friend*. Stop at the point where Franklin first sees the moose family and races home. Distribute a large sheet of paper folded in four to each student. Ask students to draw a picture of this scene in the first section of their paper. After students have drawn their pictures, discuss what Franklin might be feeling. Invite students to pretend they are Franklin. On the board, record his possible feelings using words or stick drawings. Distribute a feeling bubble to each student, who are to show Franklin's feelings using a simple picture or by printing key words in the bubble. Ask students to paste the bubble to Franklin's chest. Repeat the process, this time focussing on Franklin's thoughts.

Explore reasons

➤ Invite students to share and explain their pictures, especially the words and pictures inside their bubbles. As they share their ideas, ask them to explain why Franklin would be feeling and thinking in this way. Help students recall the story if they have difficulty offering a reason (e.g., Franklin was surprised because "the beds were made for giants," Franklin was scared because the story said so). Encourage students to find a reason from the story to explain what they put in their bubbles.

reasons

Practice finding reasons

➤ Continue reading the story to the point where recess ends and Moose gets a ball out of the tree. In the second quarter of their paper, ask students to sketch what happened when Moose came to school. Invite them to include Moose in their picture with a feeling and a thinking bubble just as they did for Franklin. Guide students by asking: "How is Moose feeling? What is he thinking? What reasons can you find in the story that tell you why Moose might feel and think this way?"

Continue with the story

➤ Continue reading the story from "Back in the classroom..." to the point where lunch ends. Ask students "What is Mr. Owl trying to do? How is Franklin feeling? What if Mr. Owl had not told Franklin to think about how Moose was feeling?" Invite students to use the third section of their paper to draw what has happened in this part of the story. Encourage students to use bubbles to show several characters' thoughts and feelings. Prompt students with questions such as "Has Franklin changed his mind about Moose? What reasons can you find in the story? What caused Franklin to change his mind about Moose?"

Identify needs

➤ Finish reading the story. In the last quarter of their paper, ask students to draw a picture with accompanying bubbles that shows something Moose needed at his new school (e.g., to be included in the soccer game at recess, to work with Franklin, to eat lunch with the other children). As they share their pictures, explore their reasons for the thoughts and feelings they imagine. Discuss the needs raised by this story by asking such questions as "What if Franklin had not thought about it and had not included Moose? What would Moose have thought and felt about school then?" Conclude by discussing how Franklin helped Moose meet his needs, and how Franklin and Moose might have felt about this.

Session Two

Recall the Franklin story

➤ Assist students in recalling the story of *Franklin's New Friend*. Refer students to the fourth drawing they sketched of the things that Moose needed at school. Ask students if Moose met these needs all by himself or if he had help in meeting them. Create a list of the names of the people who helped Moose and, in another column, list what each person did to help Moose.

Who helped	How did they help?

➤ After students offer their suggestions, you may want to reread the story, inviting students to listen for other people who helped Moose at school and how they helped him. Add these answers to the chart. Alternatively, complete the left-hand column of the chart by adding the names of all the other characters in the story (Franklin, Moose, Moose's mother and father, Franklin's mother and father, Mr. Owl, Bear, Beaver, Fox, Raccoon, Rabbit). Invite students to recall what, if anything, these people did to help Moose at school.

Introduce responsibilities

➤ When the discussion and chart are completed, ask students to imagine that they are lost and a police officer walks by. Would students expect the police officer to help them? Elicit why students think that the police officer should help them. Repeat a few other examples of obvious role responsibilities (e.g., Would they expect a family member to give food to a child who is hungry? A doctor to help someone who is very sick?). Help students understand that these people have a job (duty or special responsibility) to help in these cases. Remind students of the examples of what is "fair to expect" of objects (that a pencil will write, a book will have words or pictures). When people are in need, it is fair to expect that other people will help them. Introduce the term "responsibility," if it has not already entered the discussion, suggesting that some people have a responsibility to help others in need.

➤ Return students' attention to the list of characters who helped Moose. Select a character and ask students if the person helped Moose just because he or she wanted to, or if Moose had a right to expect that this person would help him. Guide students to see that some people have a responsibility to help meet people's needs and others may not—they may help just because they want to or they may not help out at all. Now, invite students to think of why someone has a responsibility to help and why others do not have this responsibility. Suggest several characters who also might have helped Moose meet a particular need. For example, might Mr. Owl or Moose's mother also have helped Moose? Create a chart, such as the one below, identifying one of Moose's needs, and listing several characters— some of whom might have helped and others who clearly could not have helped, perhaps because they were not at school or they did not know the children in the class. In the discussion of who has a responsibility to help meet Moose's need and why, draw out two key factors: people have a responsibility only if they are able to help, and if it is expected that they will help (i.e., if it is their job or duty, as it was for Franklin who was assigned the task of looking after Moose). Record the two criteria—able to help and expected to help—across the top of the chart and place check marks or crosses as students indicate which of the listed characters meet these criteria. After some discussion, offer up another of Moose's needs and repeat the procedure to determine who has a responsibility to help out.

criteria for responsibility

Who has a responsibility?

Moose needed…	Who might help?	Are they able to help?	Are they expected to help? (Is it their job?)
to meet new friends at school	*Franklin*	✔	✔
	Moose's mother	✗	✗
	Mr. Owl	✔	✔

➤ OPTIONAL: If the topic arises in students' discussions, you might touch upon the idea that some people may have a greater responsibility to help than other people. Mr. Owl, for example, may have been more responsible for Moose than others because he was the teacher (that is his role) and Franklin may have more responsibility to Moose than other students because he was assigned to be Moose's buddy (it was Franklin's role in this story). Two criteria for determining greater responsibility are: who is better able to help out and who might we more expect to help because it is their job or they have a special duty.

Invite students to discuss who might have the greater responsibility to help them with a very difficult arithmetic problem: The teacher? A best friend? A student who is not good in arithmetic? Or a student who they do not know very well?

Confirm understanding of concepts

➤ Confirm students' understanding of who might have a responsibility to help a person in need by inviting them to answer the questions on *Who has a responsibility?* (Blackline Master #19A–B). You may carry out this task orally with the entire class by reading the need in question and the description of the persons that students are to consider as possible helpers. Ask if each person is able to help and expected to help. Direct students to indicate yes with a "thumbs up" or no with a "thumbs down." Alternatively, provide each student with a copy of Blackline Master #19A–B and lead them through the task, inviting them to circle "YES" or "NO" for each criterion. Discuss the answers for the first question. Once students understand the task, read the descriptions of the people who might help, present the criteria using the sentence frames provided, and ask students to circle the correct answer. If some students are not able to work independently with the sheet, scribe their responses.

Name: _____

Who has a responsibility?

Blackline Master #19A

Imagine you have been asked by your teacher to bring back to your classroom a big box of books that is too heavy for you to carry. You think of three people who might have a responsibility to help you...

	Is _____ able to help you?	Is it fair to expect that _____ should help you?
A teacher who is standing just beside the box	YES NO	YES NO
Your friend who is sick at home	YES NO	YES NO
A big boy who is very strong who has been sent with you by your teacher to help carry the box	YES NO	YES NO

Rights, Roles and Responsibilities

88

TC² The Critical Thinking Cooperative

Reinforce concepts

➤ Enlarge each sheet of *Roles in school* (Blackline Master #20A–C) to ledger size (11 x 17) and cut out each role to create a large gallery display of the roles in your school. Do not display all the roles if you think students will be overwhelmed, especially since they will be asked to interview each of these people in the next critical challenge. Alternatively, you may want to create additional displays for roles not represented in Blackline Master #20, so as to introduce students to every role in your school. If you have photographs of people in various roles, attach these to the display. Introduce students to each role by pointing to a display and asking students to name the person(s) in your school who has (have) this role. Print the name(s) under the graphic on the line provided. Ask students to brainstorm what each role is responsible for in the school. Record the responsibilities on paper or index cards and place them in the display under the appropriate role.

knowledge of school roles and responsibilities

Review roles and personnel

➤ Draw students' attention to the gallery of roles and ask students to re-introduce one of the roles, using the following sentence frame:

This is   <u>(the secretary)</u>   ; his/her/their name(s) is/are <u>   </u> .
          role   *name*

One of the   <u>(secretary's)</u>   responsibilities is to <u>(answer the</u> <u>school phone)</u>.

Proceed until every student has introduced a role.

Explore role responsibilities

➤ Refer students to the four "rights" charts (safety, health, learning and happiness). Select one of the index cards with a need that would be met at school (e.g., need a hug when sad, need help when lost) and ask students to think of who in the school might have a responsibility to help them meet this need. Invite students to suggest a few names and ask them why they think this person has this responsibility. If needed, remind students of how they decided who had a responsibility to help Moose in the Franklin story. Point out the two conditions for deciding if someone has a responsibility to us: the person is able and is expected to help. Create a chart such as the one on the next page, with the title "Who is responsible for helping?" Beneath, print the words "At school we need…" and attach the index card with the need that students are considering. Below this, create two columns labeled "Is able to help us" and "Is expected to help us." Finally bring out two complete sets of role cards which you have cut out from photocopies (enlarged to 11 x 17) of *Role cards* (Blackline Master #22). One at a time, hold up each role card and ask students if this person is able to help meet the identified need. If students agree that the person is able, paste the card in the "Is able to help us" column. If students decide that the person is unable to help, place the card face down next to you. Repeat this procedure with the second set of cards to indicate who should be expected to help. When all the role cards are reviewed, ask students to indicate which roles are responsible for helping. Help students see that only if the same role card appears in both columns can they conclude that the person has a responsibility to help. Select an additional need at school and repeat the procedure.

Role cards

Blackline Master #22

Principal

Teacher

Librarian

Noon-hour supervisor

Custodian

Crossing guard

Student

Secretary

Parent volunteer

Teaching assistant

Rights, Roles and Responsibilities

94

 The Critical Thinking Cooperative

Who is responsible for helping?

At school, we need…

Is able to help us	**Is expected to help us**

Present the challenge

➤ Invite each student to select a need, perhaps the learning need each identified as the most important on Blackline Master #16 or simply pick a need at school from the "rights" charts. Alternatively, you may want to ask everyone to consider the same need, at least for the time students address this challenge. Provide each student (or pair of students) with an enlarged copy (11 x 17) of *Who is responsible for helping?* (Blackline Master #21). Ask students to draw and label the need in the box titled "At school, we need…." Present the critical question:

Who has a responsibility to help us meet this need?

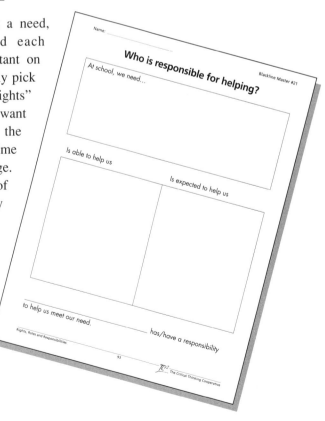

Distribute two sets of role cards (Blackline Master #21) photocopied on different coloured paper. Ask students to cut out one set of role cards and sort them into two piles: those who are able to help meet this need and those who are not able to help. When completed, invite students to paste only the "is able" roles onto Blackline Master #22. Repeat the procedure for the "is expected" requirement. Ask students to print (or scribe for them) the people who have a responsibility to help them meet the need (i.e., those people whose names appear in both columns). Encourage students to share their responses with other students and give reasons for their conclusions.

Add to roles gallery

➤ OPTIONAL: You may want to add any new responsibilities identified by students in this challenge to the lists of responsibilities found under each role on the gallery display. Add to these lists on a regular basis as students learn more about the many responsibilities carried out by school personnel.

Repeat the challenge

➤ Treat students' first effort at this challenge as a practise opportunity. Asking students to repeat the challenge several times may increase their understanding of the concept of responsibility, their knowledge of school roles and their ability to use criteria to make judgments. As well, it may be informative for students to revisit their initial conclusions about who has certain responsibilities after they learn more about each role in Critical Challenge #7.

Evaluation

Blackline Masters #23–24

Assess perspective taking

➤ Assess student's ability to imagine the thoughts and feelings of others using the rubric *Assessing perspective taking* (Blackline Master #23). The evidence for this assessment is students' drawings and their feeling and thinking bubbles from the Franklin story. Reaching the "basic understanding" level on the rubric may be appropriate for many early primary students.

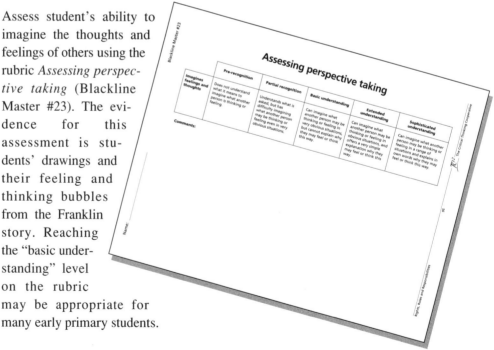

➤ Assess students' understanding of the criteria for responsibility and their knowledge of school roles and their responsibilities using the rubric *Assessing roles and responsibilities* (Blackline Master #24). The sources of evidence and the criteria for this assessment are as follows:

- use students' ability to use the sentence frame to identify responsibilities associated with particular roles to assess their knowledge of the roles and responsibilities of school members;

- use students' responses on *Who has a responsibility?* (Blackline Master #19) and *Who is responsible for helping?* (Blackline Master # 21) to assess students' ability to judge a person's responsibility in a given situation.

Reaching the "basic understanding" level on the rubric may be appropriate for many early primary students.

Extension

➤ On a regular basis, use actual incidents where someone in the school is in need as an opportunity to invite students to decide who within the school might have a responsibility to help.

References

Brownlie, Faye. et al. (1990). *Tomorrow's Classroom Today.* Pembroke. (ISBN 0-921217-50-1)

Bourgeois, Paulette. (1997). *Franklin's New Friend* (illustrated by Brenda Clark). Toronto: Kids Can Press. (ISBN 1-55074-363-5)

Meeting our needs

Critical Challenge

Critical question What is the most important responsibility of the person in this role?

Overview This challenge broadens students' understanding of the roles and responsibilities in their school. From interviews conducted with school personnel, students learn that people in various school roles are responsible for helping meet their diverse needs. After examining the responsibilities of an assigned role, students select four important responsibilities and decide which of these responsibilities is the most important in terms of students' needs. Finally, students send a note of appreciation to each person interviewed, acknowledging their help and expressing special thanks for carrying out the most important responsibility attached to their role.

Objectives

Broad understanding Many people are responsible for ensuring that students' needs at school are met.

Requisite tools *Background knowledge*
- knowledge of responsibilities related to roles

Criteria for judgment
- criteria for important responsibility (e.g. able to help, expected to help)

Critical thinking vocabulary

Thinking strategies
- interview format

Habits of mind

Suggested Activities

Pre-planning

Decide on interview details

➤ In Session Three, students interview school personnel about their roles and responsibilities. You will need to decide how many roles to involve, when and where the interviews will be conducted, and what support students will need. The entire class could interview all the roles selected or groups of students could each interview a person in a different role. You may want a combination of these options, with the entire class interviewing people in the key roles (e.g., teacher and principal). Since we include students when we list the roles in school, we suggest that the student interview be treated as a practice interview to be conducted between pairs of students. We have assumed that one teacher will represent the teacher role; alternatively, each group could interview a different teacher. Consider arranging for parents or older student helpers to bring students to and from the interviews and to assist in recording interviewee responses. Be sure to confirm the willingness and availability of potential interviewees well in advance, and provide them with a copy of the questions prior to the actual interview.

Session One *Blackline Master #25*

Introduce interview project

➤ Invite the class to think back to any instances where students disagreed about the responsibilities carried out by a particular role or expressed uncertainty over who might assist them with a particular need. Alternatively, create curiosity by asking if students know much about what the librarian or the principal do all day or who in the school has responsibilities for student safety or health. Invite the class to consider how they might find answers to questions they have about any school personnel. Guide students to the conclusion that they could ask people about their jobs and, in particular, about how these people help students meet their needs.

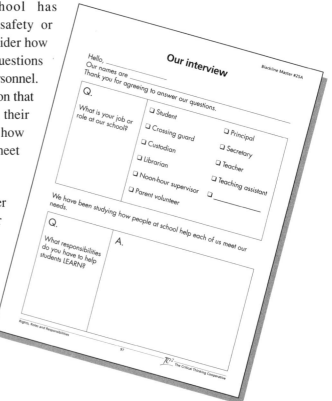

Discuss interview questions

➤ Explain to the class that in order to find answers to their questions and to better know the people in the school, the class will talk to each person about their role and how they help meet students' needs to learn and to be safe, happy and healthy. To do this, students will need to think about the information they would like to know and plan the questions to ask in order to get this information. Indicate that asking people prepared questions is called an interview. Invite students to suggest questions they might want to ask. Record their suggestions and encourage them to think of what they might ask to better understand the responsibilities that these people have to help students meet four types of needs. Explain to students that their ideas will help you prepare a list of questions. Before the next session, prepare these questions using *Our interview* (Blackline Master #25A–B) as a template. We recommend that the core questions deal with each role's responsibilities. Revise or add questions based on students' suggestions.

Session Two   *Blackline Master #25*

Explain the interview form

➤ Distribute a completed copy (enlarged to 11 x 17) of Blackline Master #25A–B (or the interview form you have developed) to each student. Read the questions and explain where and how students can record the person's responses. Reassure students that they will be able to record information in drawings or in words, and that there will be someone to scribe for them or help them write words.

Conduct student interviews

➤ Place students into pairs. Where possible, place students who are able to print with those who are not yet able. Ask students to take turns interviewing each other, using the template to guide their questions and to record their responses. It may be especially helpful to arrange for several student or parent volunteers to assist students in recording the responses. You may want to conduct these interviews in unison by reading aloud the first question and allowing time for students to respond and record, before proceeding with the second question and so on. This process must be repeated to allow both students in each pair to be interviewed. Afterwards, invite a few students to share the information they collected.

Session Three   *Blackline Master #25*

Implement interview plan

➤ On the day of the scheduled interviews, explain to students your plan for conducting the interviews. Provide each group with a fresh enlarged copy of Blackline Master #25A–B (or your own interview form). Designate those students in each group who are most able to scribe or draw as the recorders, while the other students may ask the questions. Allow time for the interview groups to meet and practice prior to their scheduled interviews.

Share information

➤ After all groups have conducted their interviews, ask each group to present its information to the class. Ask each group to start by stating the person's name, where the interview took place, and the person's role in the school. Each group member could take a turn reporting on one of the questions. If desired, ask each group to add any newly revealed responsibilities to the appropriate list of role responsibilities posted on the gallery display.

Build knowledge of role responsibilities

➤ OPTIONAL: If some students need to build their knowledge of the responsibilities of different roles in the school, bring these students to the gallery of roles and ask them to use the following sentence frames to introduce various members of the school community:

This is   (the secretary)   ; his/her/their name(s) is/are   .
          role   *name*

One of the   (secretary's)   responsibilities is to (answer the school phone).

Select four important responsibilities

➤ Organize students according to the person they interviewed. Ask them as a group or in pairs to pick four important responsibilities that this person carries out. You may need to make additional copies of the completed interview sheets if dividing the group into pairs. Distribute with each set of completed interview sheets, four stars or other small stickers. Direct students to place a sticker next to the four most important responsibilities that this person has. Remind students of the factors they considered when deciding their most important need: how often the need arose and how badly it would be missed. Encourage students to think of these two questions as they discuss the importance of each responsibility.

criteria for important responsibility

Present critical challenge

➤ When students have identified four important responsibilities, present the critical question:

> *What is the most important responsibility of the person in this role?*

Encourage students to think about the two questions mentioned above as they discuss their answer: "Which of their responsibilities is needed most often?" and "Which of their responsibilities would be most missed if they were not carried out?"

Prepare note of appreciation

➤ Once each group has selected four important responsibilities and then chosen which of these is the most important, distribute an enlarged copy (11 x 17) of *Note of appreciation* (Blackline Master #26) to each group (or pair of students). Explain that they will prepare and send a note of appreciation to the person they interviewed to thank the person for helping to meet their needs. Help students understand what they are to print or have scribed. Remind them to state three important responsibilities. For the most important responsibility, students are to state the need that this responsibility helps to meet (e.g., safety, health).

When the written part is completed, ask each student to draw a picture of the person performing his or her most important responsibility. Distribute a piece of paper approximately the size of the box on Master #26 to ensure that the pictures will fit on the note of appreciation. Allow students to choose which of their pictures will be pasted in the box (and attach the others to the note) or suggest that students pick a number to decide. Send the notes when completed.

Note of appreciation
Blackline Master #26

To: _____
Role: _____
School: _____

_____

We appreciate many things that you do to help us meet our needs:

1. _____
2. _____
3. _____

But we REALLY appreciate how you help us meet our need to _____
when you _____
Thank you very, very much.

Signed _____

Rights, Roles and Responsibilities

99

TC^2 The Critical Thinking Cooperative

Assess roles and responsibilities

➤ Assess students' knowledge of school roles and their responsibilities using the rubric *Assessing roles and responsibilities* (Blackline Master #24). The source of evidence is students' ability to use the sentence frame to identify responsibilities associated with particular school roles. Reaching the "basic understanding" level on the rubric may be appropriate for many early primary students.

Assess important responsibilities

➤ Assess students' understanding of the important role responsibilities using the rubric *Assessing important needs and responsibilities* (Blackline Master #17). The sources of evidence for this assessment are the starred responsibilities on the interview copy of *Our interview* (Blackline Master #25) and student responses on *Note of appreciation* (Blackline Master #26).

Guess who?

Critical Challenge

Critical question   Who has these responsibilities at our school?

Overview   In this challenge, students extend their knowledge of the responsibilities attached to different roles in their school by creating and solving riddles about each role. Students are introduced to a technique for solving riddles and to a four-part structure for developing riddles. Students exchange their completed interview information from the previous challenge with other students who then develop a riddle based on the most important responsibilities attached to the role. After learning about "reasonable guesses," students try to solve the riddles presented to them.

Objectives

Broad understanding   Many people are responsible for ensuring that students' needs at school are met; some responsibilities are unique to a role and others are shared by people in many roles.

Requisite tools

Background knowledge
- knowledge of riddles
- knowledge of responsibilities related to roles

Criteria for judgment
- criteria for a reasonable guess (e.g., fits the clue)

Critical thinking vocabulary
- clues

Thinking strategies
- riddle chart
- elimination of possible guesses

Habits of mind

Suggested Activities

Introduce riddles

➤ Begin by inviting students to present any riddles they know to the class. If no one has a riddle or after students have volunteered them, present a riddle of your own that has four clues, as suggested by the following example:

knowledge of riddles

> I have four legs.
>
> I like to live in a house with people.
>
> I wag my tail when I am happy.
>
> Sometimes I chase cats.
>
> What am I?

Introduce clues

➤ After students solve your riddle, ask them to tell you the first clue you offered. Check that students understand what a clue is—information that helps one guess what an answer might be. Inquire if anyone knew it was a dog after this first clue. Invite students to suggest what else they thought it could be (e.g., mouse, cat, dog, horse, pig, cow, gerbil). Record possible guesses in a row across the top of the board or chart paper, using the format below. Ask students to explain why the secret animal could not have been a bird or a spider. Turn to the second clue and ask students, "What might it be after this clue?" The guesses from the first clue that fit the second clue should be copied to the second row of the chart. Point out that by giving additional information, the second clue helps to get rid of some guesses. Continue this procedure with the next two clues, emphasizing the continual elimination of guesses (and possibly the addition of new ones not previously imagined).

clue

eliminating guesses

Solving a riddle

Possible guesses								
Clue 1: mouse	cat	dog	horse	pig	gerbil	frog	elephant	tiger
Clue 2:	mouse		cat		dog		gerbil	
Clue 3:		cat (maybe)			dog			
Clue 4:				dog				

**Model the
riddle game**

➤ Ask students if they would
like to play a riddle game
about people in the school.
Distribute an enlarged
copy (11 x 17) of
Guesses (Blackline Master #27) and a set of
role cards (Blackline
Master #21) to each
pair of students. Ask
students to cut out
the role cards. Explain that you will
present a riddle
about one of the
roles on these
cards. Select a
riddle from *Practice riddles*
(Blackline Master #28) or create
your own four-clue riddle about a
role in your school. If making
you own riddles, minimize the
use of clues dealing with role
responsibilities since students
will be asked to make up their
own riddles with responsibilities as the focus for their
clues. Read out the first
clue of your chosen riddle
and ask students to place
all the role cards that are
possible guesses in the top
row of Blackline Master #27. When students have done this, agree as a class on the guesses
that fit the clue. Encourage students to add role cards they may
have overlooked or to take away others that do not fit the clue. Read
the second clue and ask students to place onto the second row all the
cards from the top row that fit this second clue. As before, confirm
that all students have selected the correct role cards. Repeat the procedure with the remaining two clues, emphasizing the importance of
ensuring that the guesses fit the clue.

**Practise
solving riddles**

➤ Offer students several more riddles drawn from (Blackline Master
#28) to practise the riddle game. Until students master the strategy,
continue to confirm after each clue that all students have placed the
correct role cards in the appropriate row.

Create the riddles

➤ When students are familiar with use of the role cards and the guesses chart to solve riddles, ask students if they would like to make riddles of their own for the rest of the class to guess. Distribute to each pair of students either a copy of a completed interview (Blackline Master #24A–B) or a note of appreciation (Blackline Master #25) for different people. Emphasize that students must not tell other students the name of their mystery role. Distribute a copy of *Creating a riddle* (Blackline Master #29) to each pair of students. Ask students to select four responsibilities from the interview sheet as the source of clues for their riddle. Model how they might do this using a completed student interview. Look for a responsibility on the interview sheet (e.g., I have a responsibility to help students who ask me) and indicate how you would use this information to complete the sentence for the first clue "One of my responsibilities is...." Help students transfer the information from the interview sheet or the note of appreciation to the clue format. While doing so, make sure that the sequence of clues is such that the clues that apply most broadly come first, and the more specific clues come later. You may want to review and edit each riddle prior to using it with the class.

knowledge of responsibilities

riddle chart

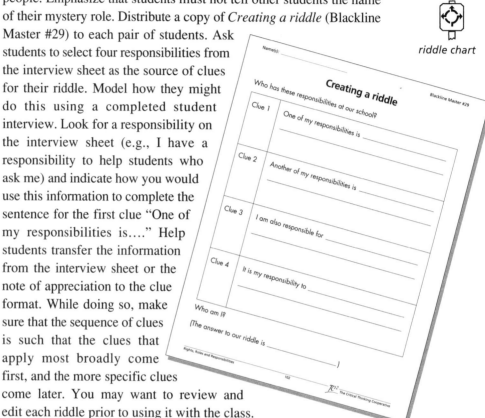

Present the challenge

➤ After you have reviewed each student-developed set of clues to ensure that they will provide a successful riddle, return the riddles to their creators and invite them, in turn, to present the critical question:

Who has these responsibilities at our school?

➤ Arrange for each pair of students to alternate reading a clue, allowing time for the rest of the class to place the role cards on the guesses chart. Allow every pair to present its riddle, although you may want to spread this activity over several sessions. If you want a record of students' performance on the riddles, distribute additional copies of the role cards (Blackline Master #21) and guesses chart (Blackline Master #27) and ask students, after each clue, to paste the role cards or to print the names of the role on the appropriate rows.

**Assess knowledge
of role responsibilities**

➤ Assess students' knowledge of school roles and their responsibilities using the rubric *Assessing roles and responsibilities* (Blackline Master #24). The source of evidence is students' responses to the clues for each school role, either as observed during the solving of riddles or as recorded by students on *Guesses* (Blackline Master #27).

**Assess solving
of role riddles**

➤ Assess students' ability to recognize and offer reasonable guesses and to decide upon a best guess after hearing the clues using the rubric *Assessing guesses* (Blackline Master #30). The source of evidence is students' responses to the clues for each school role, either as observed during the solving of riddles or as recorded by students on *Guesses* (Blackline Master #27).

sorting

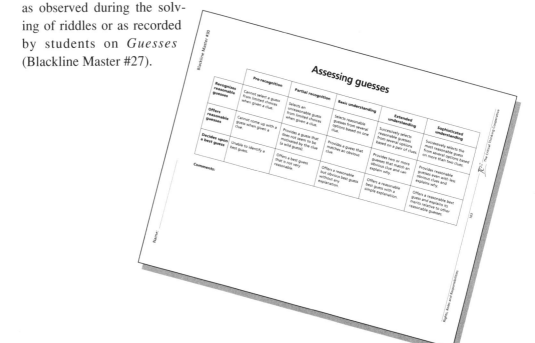

How responsible am I?

Critical Challenge

Critical task/question
A. Choose two important personal responsibilities at school: a responsibility to help others and a responsibility to help yourself.

B. How well do you meet your two responsibilities: most of the time, some of the time, or not very often?

Overview
In this challenge, students move from examining the responsibilities that others have to help them, to their own responsibilities to help themselves and others. A Shel Silverstein poem explores the consequences when someone does not carry out their responsibilities. Students also consider that their responsibilities include a responsibility to help themselves meet their needs. Using previously developed lists of important needs at school, students select two important responsibilities—one involving a responsibility to themselves and another a responsibility to others. Students clarify what these responsibilities require and then look to see how well they carry out these responsibilities. Based on evidence collected, students assess how responsible they are and what they might do to increase their level of personal responsibility.

Objectives

Broad understanding
Each of us has responsibilities to help meet our own needs and the needs of others.

Requisite tools

Background knowledge
- knowledge of needs and responsibilities

Criteria for judgment
- criteria for important personal responsibility (e.g., is a problem, able to do something, am expected to try, would make a big difference)
- criteria for responsible behaviour (e.g., consistently carries out one's responsibilities)

Critical thinking vocabulary
- evidence

Thinking strategies
- elimination of options
- evidence chart

Habits of mind
- honest, thoughtful response

Suggested Activities

Pre-planning

➤ In this two-part challenge, students explore how responsible they are in carrying out two kinds of expected duties: responsibilities to help other students and responsibilities to make sure their own needs are met. We suggest that you identify approximately five responsibilities of each type (self and other) that would make a suitable range of options from which students will select. For Session Two, you will need to complete and duplicate *Responsibility cards* (Blackline Master #31) for each of these identified responsibilities. Students will use these cards to select the most important responsibilities for them to examine.

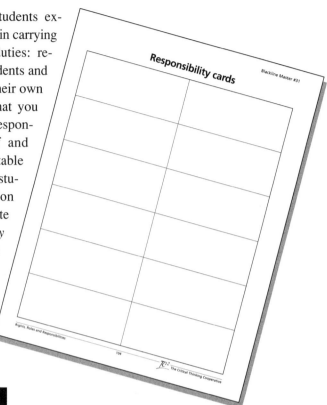

Session One

➤ Explain to students you are going to read a poem about someone who has a job to do. Before reading it, ask students what jobs young people like themselves can do at home. Brainstorm a list of familiar jobs (e.g., feeding a pet, making their bed, washing dishes). Label this list, "Our responsibilities at home." Discuss what happens if they do not do their job (meet their responsibilities). Read the poem, "Sarah Cynthia Sylvia Stout Would Not Take the Garbage Out" by S. Silverstein (see References). Afterwards, ask students to identify Sarah's job (responsibility) and what happened when she did not carry it out. Draw out that each us of has jobs to do—responsibilities to carry out—and that an unwillingness to do them can cause problems.

*knowledge of
responsibilities*

➤ Create a new column with the title, "Our responsibilities at school" and invite students to brainstorm the jobs they have as students (e.g., listen carefully, try their best, take part in activities). When students exhaust their ideas, direct their attention to the lists and charts of important needs at school generated in earlier sessions. Recall for students the meaning of "responsibilities" as those things that must be done in order to meet people's needs. Ask students if they have any responsibilities to help others meet these needs (e.g., a need to have hugs, a need to help others who are lost). Remind students that they earlier decided who had responsibilities to help them by judging

*knowledge
of needs*

whether the person was able to help and was expected to help. Help students draw out personal responsibilities from the needs listed on the charts and depicted in their drawings. Ask, for example, "If we need a safe classroom, what responsibilities might we have in meeting this need?" Where possible, direct students' attention towards responsibilities that are on your list of responsibilities that you will want students to self-assess later in the challenge. Add new responsibilities to the list as students acknowledge them. Conclude the session by asking students two questions:

- How well are you meeting all your responsibilities?

- How do you know if your are meeting them?

Announce that the next day students will ask themselves the question "How responsible am I?"

Session Two

Blackline Masters #27, 31–32

Present the responsibilities to others

➤ Draw students' attention to the list, "Our responsibilities at school." Explain that you think it would be beneficial for the class to focus on five (or six) responsibilities that all or most students in the class share. Point to these on the list. Briefly discuss what each means and what it would look and sound like to meet each responsibility.

Present first part of challenge

➤ Suggest to the class that over the next few days, each student will pay careful attention to how responsible he or she is in carrying out one of these responsibilities. To begin with, each student must decide on a focus by answering the first critical task:

Choose an [important] responsibility to help others...

To help students decide on an important responsibility, the class will play the riddle game, except that the "right" answer will depend upon the individual student. Give each student a copy of *Guesses* (Blackline Master #27). Also distribute the strip of five or six responsibilities that you identified and recorded on the blank responsibility cards (Blackline Master #31). Ask students to cut out the cards. Explain that you will present "clues" (criteria) to help students decide which of the responsibilities on the cards might be an important responsibility for each student to explore further. As you present the following clues, allow time for students to place and move the appropriate cards onto each row:

- *clue 1:* This a problem for students in our class.

- *clue 2:* You are able to do something to help others.

- *clue 3:* You are expected to try to help.

- *clue 4:* It would make things much better if you helped.

criteria for important personal responsibility

elimination of options

Even after the fourth clue, some students may have more than one choice. In which case, encourage them to choose one of the remaining possibilities. Alternatively, reread the clues for these students, encouraging them to double-check that each possibility fits the clues.

Record their choices

➤ When students have made their decision, ask them to glue the cards in the rows where they appeared after the last round of clues. In addition, distribute the first page of *How responsible am I?* (Blackline Master #32A). Ask students to draw a picture of themselves carrying out the chosen responsibility. This drawing belongs in the top box of Blackline Master #32A.

Name: _____

How responsible am I?

Blackline Master #32A

I have a responsibility to help other students _____

I have a responsibility to help myself by _____

Rights, Roles and Responsibilities

105

TC² The Critical Thinking Cooperative

Session Three   *Blackline Masters #27 & 31*

Introduce responsibilities to help themselves

➤ Explain to the class that not only does each person have responsibilities to other people, each of us has responsibilities to ourself. Invite students to consider what these might be by selecting a simple responsibility from the "Our responsibilities at school" list. Refer, for example, to the responsibility to give hugs to people who are lonely. Students can help others meet this need by giving them hugs, but they also can help with their own need for hugs. Ask students the following question: "Who gets more hugs? Someone who is nice to her friends or someone who is mean to them?" Use their answers to illustrate that students can contribute to their own need for hugs by treating people nicely. Present other examples of ways in which students can contribute to meeting their own needs. The following suggestions may help:

Our need	How we can help ourselves meet this need
• the need for help when we are stuck	• letting others know when we are stuck
• the need for fun time	• doing assigned our work when asked
• the need for smiles	• smiling to others

sorting

Present the responsibilities to ourselves

➤ When students appreciate that they do have a responsibility to help themselves, introduce the five responsibilities that you have selected for students to examine. (These should be widely shared and perhaps not well-fulfilled by students.) Point to these on the list "Our responsibilities at school." Briefly discuss what each means and what it might look and sound like to meet this responsibility to themselves.

Present second part of challenge

➤ Suggest that for the next few days, students will pay careful attention to how responsible they are in meeting one of their responsibilities to themselves. Invite students to select the responsibility they wish to focus upon by presenting the final part of the first critical task:

Choose a [important] responsibility to help yourself.

Follow the same procedure as the previous day. Distribute a copy of Blackline Master #27 and the strip of five or six responsibilities created from Blackline Master #31. After students cut out the cards, proceed with the following "clues," allowing time for students to place the appropriate cards on each row:

- *clue 1:* Is a problem for you in school.

- *clue 2:* You are able to do something to help yourself.

- *clue 3:* You are expected to try to help yourself.

- *clue 4:* It would make things much better for you if you tried.

Record their choices

➤ Follow a similar procedure for helping all students reach a decision and for pasting their guesses on the chart. Point out the box on the bottom half of Blackline Master #32A and ask students to draw a picture of themselves carrying out their chosen responsibility.

Session Four *Blackline Master #32*

Organize support teams

➤ Once every student has two responsibilities to investigate, explain how they will gather information about how responsible they are. Organize students into teams of three. Explain that the team's job is to help each member decide whether or not he or she is acting responsibly. To begin, suggest that team members share and discuss their pictures so that everyone understands the responsibilities that each team member has chosen. Next distribute the three remaining sheets in *How responsible am I?* (Blackline Master #32B–D). Help students create a booklet from these sheets with the drawings serving as a cover page.

Review the responsibilities

➤ Direct students to the boxes on the very top of the second and third pages of their booklets (Blackline Master #32B–C). Invite students to work through each of their responsibilities, identifying what this responsibility might look or sound like. If students are unfamiliar with this strategy, explore several responsibilities with the entire class. Explain that students will use the next two boxes on the second and third pages of their booklet (showing a happy and sad face) to record when they act in ways that meet their two responsibilities (I did this when… and when they do not act responsibly (I did not do this when…).

Establish the period for investigation

➤ Allow students sufficient opportunity to try to carry out their responsibilities over the rest of the day and perhaps on the following day. At a convenient time, invite each team to look at what each member has recorded as evidence for each responsibility.

Session Five	Blackline Master #32

Introduce the critical question

➤ When sufficient time has elapsed, present the critical question to each student:

How well did you meet your two responsibilities: most of the time, some of the time, or not very often?

Each student is to judge how regularly they met their two responsibilities and to record their assessments on the bottom box on the second and third pages of their booklet. Encourage students to base their assessment on the information they collected about their behaviour. Suggest that team members consult with one another about the most reasonable assessment.

Plan for improvement

➤ After completing these tasks for two responsibilities, invite students to complete the final page of their booklet (Blackline Master #32D) in two steps:

- indicate where they performed well and how they know this;

- identify where they could improve and how they might do this.

Students will likely need assistance from older buddies or an adult to complete these tasks. Provide an opportunity for students to share their assessments and plans for improvement with fellow students or with parents. You might want to present students with a "note of appreciation" extolling their efforts to meet their responsibilities to themselves and to others.

Assess personal responsibility

➤ Assess students' ability to identify important personal responsibilities, to collect evidence about personal behaviour and to self-assess their behaviour using the rubric *Assessing personal responsibility* (Blackline Master #33). The sources of evidence and criteria for these assessments are as follows:

- use students' selection of two important personal responsibilities and their reasoning as recorded on *Guesses* (Blackline Master #27) to assess their ability to identify important personal responsibilities;

- use students' comments about what they did and did not do as recorded on *How responsible am I?* (Blackline Master #32B–C) to assess their ability to collect evidence about personal behaviour;

- use students' assessments of their performance recorded on *How responsible am I?* (Blackline Master #32B–D) to assess their ability to judge their own behaviour.

Reaching the "basic understanding" level on the rubric may be appropriate for many early primary students.

Extension

Conduct regular self-assessments

➤ Periodically, involve students in identifying a focus for self-assessment, in gathering information and feedback and in making an assessment on the adequacy of their behaviour and, if warranted, steps for improvement.

References

Silverstein, Shel. (1974). "Sarah Cynthia Sylvia Stout Would Not Take the Garbage Out." *Where the Sidewalk Ends: The Poems and Drawings of Shel Silverstein.* New York: Harper & Row. (ISBN 06-025667-2)

List of Blackline Masters

What is needed?

Does a car  need wheels to drive?

YES   A car needs wheels because you cannot drive the car without them.

NO   It's nice to have wheels but a car does not need them because you can still drive without them.

Does a book  need pages to read?

YES   A book needs pages because you cannot read a book without pages.

NO   It's nice to have pages but a book does not need them because you can still read a book without them.

Does a pencil need an eraser to write?

YES   A pencil needs an eraser because you cannot write without it.

NO   It's nice to have an eraser but a pencil does not need it because you can still write without it.

Does a kite  need pictures  on it to fly?

YES   A kite needs pictures because you cannot fly a kite without them.

NO   It's nice to have pictures but a kite does not need them because you can still fly a kite without them.

Bicycle

TC^2 The Critical Thinking Cooperative

Parts of a bicycle

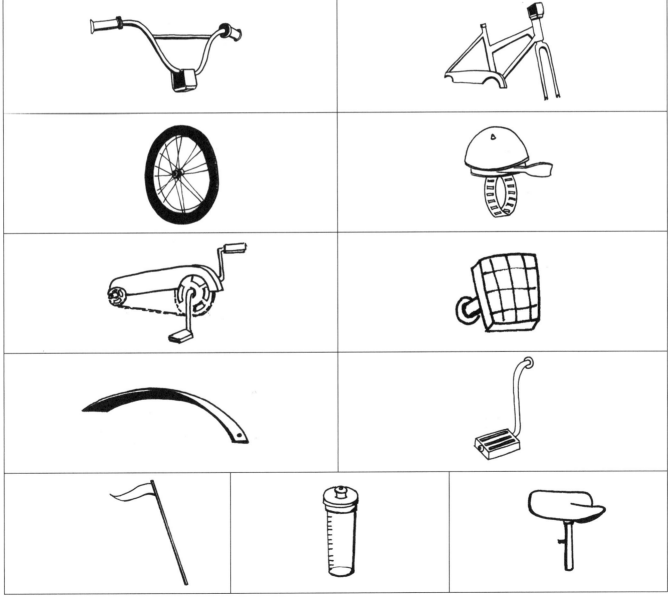

Needed or nice?

Needed	Nice to have

Parts of a car

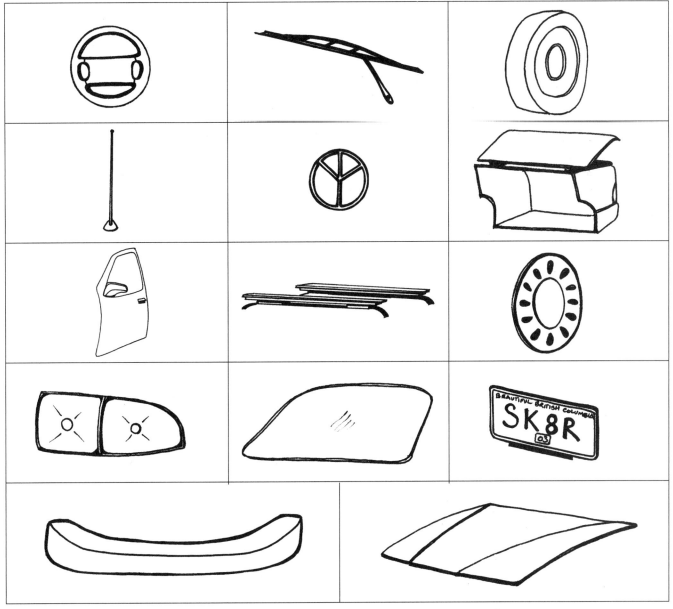

73

TC² The Critical Thinking Cooperative

Car

Driving a car

A car needs _____

because you cannot drive without it/them.

It's nice to have _____

but a car does not need it/them because you can still drive

without it/them.

A car  needs _____

because you cannot drive without it/them.

It's nice to have _____

but a car does not need it/them because you can still drive

without it/them.

Assessing needs and wants

	Pre-recognition	Partial recognition	Basic understanding	Extended understanding	Sophisticated understanding
Identifies needs for a specified object, activity or right	Does not understand what is asked when invited to identify a need associated with a designated item.	Understands what is asked, but has difficulty in identifying very obvious needs associated with a designated item.	Correctly identifies very obvious needs without explaining why they are needed.	Correctly identifies both of needs and wants, and provides an example of a clue and a guess.	Correctly identifies a range of needs and wants in own words why they are needed.
Distinguishes needs from wants	Does not understand what is asked when invited to sort needs and wants.	Understands what is asked but cannot consistently distinguish obvious examples of needs and wants.	Correctly distinguishes very obvious examples of needs and wants, but without providing any explanation.	Correctly distinguishes obvious examples of needs and wants, offering a very simple explanation.	Correctly distinguishes many examples of needs and wants, explaining the difference in their own words.

Comments:

Planning for an activity

Fun activity_____

I need to have…   It would be nice to have…

What is fair to expect?

Is it fair to expect that...

				YES	NO
a pencil		will fly		YES	NO
a lamp		will give light		YES	NO
a knife		will sing		YES	NO

Do I have a right to expect...

				YES	NO
a pencil		will swim		YES	NO
a lamp		will sing		YES	NO
a knife		will cut		YES	NO

Visiting my friend's home

My friend and I are playing at my friend's home

Fair to expect	Not fair to expect
When visiting my friend's home, I have a right to expect _____	When visiting my friend's home, I do NOT have a right to expect
_____	_____

Assessing fair expectations

	Pre-recognition	Partial recognition	Basic understanding	Extended understanding	Sophisticated understanding
Recognizes when an expectation is fair	Does not understand what is meant by a fair expectation of someone or something.	Understands what is asked, but has difficulty recognizing a fair expectation even in very obvious situations.	Recognizes fair expectations of people or things in very obvious situations without explaining why they are fair expectations.	Recognizes fair expectations of people or things in obvious situations and offers a very simple explanation why they are fair expectations.	Recognizes fair expectations of people or things across a range of situations and explains in own words why they are fair expectations.

Comments:

Rights graphics

A right to be healthy

A right to be safe

TC^2 The Critical Thinking Cooperative

A right to be happy

A right to learn

What I really need

Do we need lots of candy **to be happy** **?**

YES   We need lots of candy because we can't be happy

without it.

NO   It is nice to have lots of candy but we do not

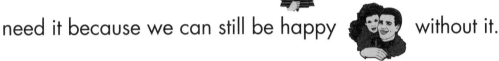need it because we can still be happy without it.

Do we need lots of fresh air **to be healthy** **?**

YES   We need lots of fresh air  because we can't be

healthy without it.

NO   It is nice to have lots of fresh air but we

do not need it because we can be healthy without it.

Do we need always to look both ways when crossing a street  **to**

be safe  **?**

YES   We need always to look both ways when crossing a street because

we can't be safe  without doing it.

NO   It is nice to always look both ways when crossing a street

but we do not need to do it because we can be safe  without

doing it.

Meeting our needs at school

Which items are…

MORE important	LESS important

What I need most so I can learn

When learning, my most important need is _____

because _____

Assessing important needs and responsibilities

	Pre-recognition	Partial recognition	Basic understanding	Extended understanding	Sophisticated understanding
Recognizes important needs and responsibilities	Does not understand what it means to judge the importance of needs or responsibilities.	Understands what is asked, but has difficulty recognizing the importance of needs and responsibilities even in very obvious situations.	Recognizes the importance of needs and responsibilities in very obvious situations without explaining why they have the importance they do.	Recognizes the importance of needs and responsibilities in obvious situations and offers a very simple explanation of their importance.	Recognizes the importance of needs and responsibilities in a range of situations and explains in own words why they have the importance they do.

Comments:

Thinking and feeling bubbles

Who has a responsibility?

Imagine you have been asked by your teacher to bring back to your classroom a big box of books that is too heavy for you to carry. You think of three people who might have a responsibility to help you…

	Is _____ able to help you?	Is it fair to expect that _____ should help you?
A teacher who is standing just beside the box	YES NO	YES NO
Your friend who is sick at home	YES NO	YES NO
A big boy who is very strong who has been sent with you by your teacher to help carry the box	YES NO	YES NO

Imagine you are in class working on an arithmetic problem that is too hard for you to do, but you must solve the problem before you go to recess. You think of three people who might have a responsibility to help you.

	Is _____ able to help you?	Is it fair to expect that _____ should help you?
Your teacher who is standing just beside you	YES NO	YES NO
Your friend who is really good at arithmetic and sits next to you	YES NO	YES NO
The person who lives next door to you, who is very good at arithmetic, but who has left town for a long trip	YES NO	YES NO

Roles in school

Principal:

_____

Crossing guard:

_____

Teacher:

_____

Student:

_____

Librarian:

_____

Secretary:

_____

Noon-hour supervisor:

_____

Parent volunteer:

_____

TC² The Critical Thinking Cooperative

Custodian:

_____

Teaching assistant:

_____

_____:

_____

_____:

_____

Who is responsible for helping?

At school, we need…

Is able to help us

Is expected to help us

_____ has/have a responsibility
to help us meet our need.

93

TC² The Critical Thinking Cooperative

Role cards

Principal

Crossing guard

Teacher

Student

Librarian

Secretary

Noon-hour supervisor

Parent volunteer

Custodian

Teaching assistant

TC² The Critical Thinking Cooperative

Assessing perspective taking

	Pre-recognition	Partial recognition	Basic understanding	Extended understanding	Sophisticated understanding
Imagines feelings and thoughts	Does not understand what it means to imagine what another person is thinking or feeling.	Understands what is asked, but has difficulty imagining what another person may be thinking or feeling even in very obvious situations.	Can imagine what another person may be thinking or feeling in very obvious situations, but cannot explain why they may feel or think this way.	Can imagine what another person may be thinking or feeling in obvious situations, and offers a very simple explanation why they may feel or think this way.	Can imagine what another person may be thinking or feeling in a range of situations and explains in own words why they may feel or think this way.

Comments:

Assessing roles and responsibilities

	Pre-recognition	Partial recognition	Basic understanding	Extended understanding	Sophisticated understanding
Knowledge of school roles	Does not understand what is asked when invited to identify a school role.	Understands what is asked but cannot correctly identify any school role.	Identifies only the most obvious school roles (e.g., teacher, principal)	Identifies the common roles in the school community.	Identifies a wide range of roles in the extended school community.
Knowledge of role responsibilities in school	Does not understand what is asked when invited to identify the responsibilities associated with a school role.	Understands what is asked but has difficulty identifying very obvious responsibilities associated with a school role.	Identifies only the most obvious responsibilities associated with a few school roles.	Identifies the main responsibilities associated with common roles in the school community.	Identifies a wide range of responsibilities associated with roles in the extended school community.
Judges a person's responsibility in a situation	Does not understand what it means to decide if someone has a responsibility in a given situation.	Understands what is asked but has difficulty in deciding if people have a responsibility, but cannot explain why they meet the identified criteria.	Can decide only in the most obvious situations if people have a responsibility, but cannot explain why they meet the identified criteria.	Can decide in obvious situations if people have a responsibility and can offer a very simple explanation why they meet the identified criteria.	Can decide in a range of situations if people have a responsibility and can explain in their own words why the individual meets the identified criteria.

Comments:

Our interview

Hello, _____

Our names are _____

Thank you for agreeing to answer our questions.

| Q.

What is your job or role at our school? | ❏ Student

❏ Crossing guard

❏ Custodian

❏ Librarian

❏ Noon-hour supervisor

❏ Parent volunteer | ❏ Principal

❏ Secretary

❏ Teacher

❏ Teaching assistant

❏ _____ |

We have been studying how people at school help each of us meet our needs.

Q. What responsibilities do you have to help students LEARN?	A.

Q. What responsibilities do you have to help students be SAFE?	A.
Q. What responsibilities do you have to help students be HEALTHY?	A.
Q. What responsibilities do you have to help students be HAPPY?	A.
Q. _____ _____ _____	A.

Thank you for answering our questions.

Note of appreciation

To: _____

Role: _____

School: _____

[ ]

We appreciate many things that you do to help us meet our needs:

1. _____

2. _____

3. _____

But we REALLY appreciate how you help us meet our need to _____

_____

when you _____

Thank you very, very much.

Signed _____

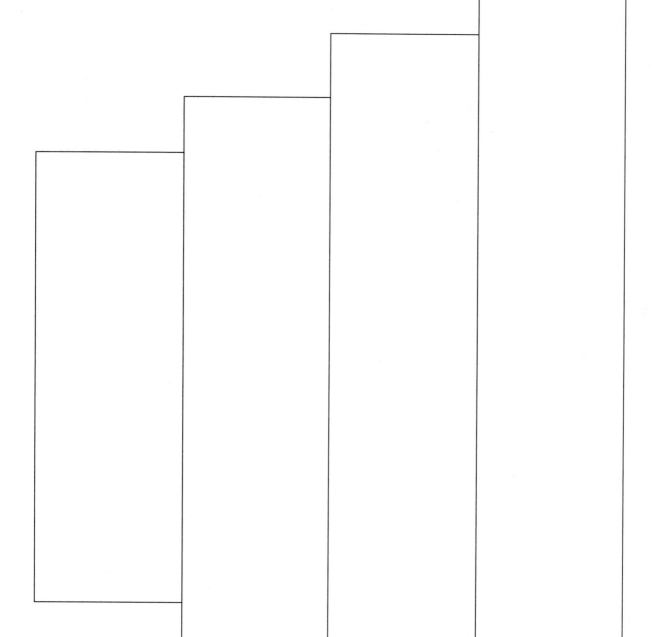

Clue 4

Clue 3

Clue 2

Clue 1

Guesses

Practice riddles

I have a desk to work at.
I like to read stories to children.
I help you find interesting books.
I scan your book before you take it away.

It is important to me that you play nicely together.
I help you if you are hurt.
I only come to school at certain times of the day.
A lot of my work is outside.

I use equipment in my work.
I work outside.
I help protect you.
You need me when you cross the street.

I work at a desk.
If you need something I am happy to help you.
People come to see me for information about the school.
I take a lot of telephone messages.

I come to school every day.
I can help people solve problems.
During the day I talk to lots of different people.
It is my responsibility to be a good learner.

I have a special room.
I appreciate it when you try to keep the school clean and neat.
I work in many different rooms in the school.
I am at school when you go home.

I will help you if you are hurt or having trouble.
I do most of my work in the same room.
I speak to you every day.
I help you learn.

Creating a riddle

Who has these responsibilities at our school?

Clue 1	One of my responsibilities is _____ _____
Clue 2	Another of my responsibilities is _____ _____
Clue 3	I am also responsible for _____ _____
Clue 4	It is my responsibility to _____ _____

Who am I?

(The answer to our riddle is _____)

Assessing guesses

	Pre-recognition	Partial recognition	Basic understanding	Extended understanding	Sophisticated understanding
Recognizes reasonable guesses	Cannot select a guess from limited choices when given a clue.	Selects an unreasonable guess from limited choices when given a clue.	Selects reasonable guesses from several options based on one clue.	Successively selects reasonable guesses from several options based on a pair of clues.	Successively selects the most reasonable guess from several options based on more than two clues.
Offers reasonable guesses	Cannot come up with a guess when given a clue.	Provides a guess that does not seem to be motivated by the clue (a wild guess).	Provides a guess that matches an obvious clue.	Provides two or more guesses that match an obvious clue and can explain why.	Provides reasonable guesses even with less obvious clues and explains why.
Decides upon a best guess	Unable to identify a best guess.	Offers a best guess that is not very reasonable.	Offers a reasonable but obvious best guess without any explanation.	Offers a reasonable best guess with a simple explanation.	Offers a reasonable best guess and explains its merits relative to other reasonable guesses.

Comments:

Responsibility cards

How responsible am I?

I have a responsibility to help other students _____

I have a responsibility to help myself by _____

	Looks like	Sounds like
Meeting my responsibility to OTHER STUDENTS		

☺ I did this when...

☹ I did not do this when...

I meet this responsibility...

❑ most of the time ★ ★ ★

❑ some of the time ★ ★

❑ not very often ★

I had help gathering information about my behaviour from my team members _____ and _____ .

	Looks like	Sounds like
Meeting my responsibility to ME		

☺ I did this when...

☹ I did not do this when...

I meet this responsibility...

- ❏ most of the time ★ ★ ★
- ❏ some of the time ★ ★
- ❏ not very often ★

I had help gathering information about my behaviour from my team members _____ and _____ .

TC² The Critical Thinking Cooperative

In thinking about how responsible I am...

☺ I am good at _____

_____

I know this because _____

_____

☹ I think I could do better at _____

_____

if I _____

_____

Assessing personal responsibility

	Pre-recognition	Partial recognition	Basic understanding	Extended understanding	Sophisticated understanding
Identifies a personal responsibility	Does not understand what is asked when invited to select an important personal responsibility.	Understands what is asked, but has difficulty selecting personal responsibilities of any importance or relevance.	Selects personal responsibilities that are important and relevant, but cannot explain why they are so.	Selects personal responsibilities that are important and relevant, and offers a very simple explanation why they are so.	Selects personal responsibilities that are obviously important and highly relevant, and explains in own words why they are so.
Collects evidence about personal behaviour	Does not understand what is meant when asked to collect evidence about personal behaviour.	Understands what is asked, but has difficulty recognizing what would count as appropriate evidence to collect.	Identifies and collects very basic, but incomplete evidence of personal behaviour.	Identifies and collects an adequate amount of evidence of personal behaviour.	Identifies and collects varied and reliable evidence of personal behaviour.
Supports assessments with evidence/ reason	Is unable to decide between assessment options.	Offers assessments but the evidence or reasons contradict or are irrelevant to the chosen options.	Offers reasonable assessments supported with very vague reasons or evidence.	Offers reasonable assessments supported with simple reasons or evidence.	Offers reasonable assessments supported with more than one reason or piece of evidence.

Comments: